To Dad
Happy Birthday
love
Annette and John

November, 1973

FLORIDA
A Picture Tour

FLORIDA

A Picture Tour

Introduction by Richard Powell

CHARLES SCRIBNER'S SONS, NEW YORK

Printed in Japan
Library of Congress Catalog Card Number 72-1184
SBN 684-13005-X

A–10.72(X)

Title page picture: The entire Florida peninsula can be seen in a photograph shot from a spacecraft.
Pictures are from the files of the Florida News Bureau, Tallahassee, with the exception of those on pages 74–75, courtesy of NASA, and pages 158-59, *Friends Magazine.*

Contents

INTRODUCTION: THE IMPROBABLE LAND   7

A HISTORICAL VIEW   21

A PICTURE TOUR   29

THE IMPROBABLE LAND

Richard Powell

It lies dreaming in the wide waters like those fabled lands of Cockaigne and Atlantis and St. Brendan's Isle and Lyonesse and Avalon. It is just as improbable a place as any of these, but it is real and carries a lovely purring name: Florida.

Even the name is improbable. It should have been called Beniny,—a harsh and tinny word—because that was the name of the place that the royal patent of Charles V authorized Ponce de Leon to discover. But when he found land the time was that of the Feast of Flowers, Pascua Florida, and for some magic reason Ponce de Leon did not give it the tinny name but a glorious scented one. He had no idea what he had found. All he could possibly have seen on that day in late March in 1513 was a white beach hedged by sea grape and the shock heads of cabbage palms. As far as he knew it might only have been a small island, making an orphan appearance on the doorstep of history. Why, then, did he ornament a possible sand bar with a jeweled title? We do not know. All we can say is that there have been many times when something in Florida's golden air bemused a practical man and entangled him in visions.

The mainland that Ponce de Leon eventually found is a large peninsula laved by warm shallow seas and toasted by almost constant sunshine. These may seem like considerable advantages, until one remembers that Baja California can be described in the same way and is mostly unlivable, and that the peninsula of Yucatan is only moderately livable, as successive Mayan civilizations learned. What makes Baja California a poor land is lack of fresh water. Yucatan gets a great deal of fresh water but loses it rapidly, due to tricks of nature. Florida is a giant sponge. It sops up enormous amounts of fresh water, storing it in 30,000 lakes and in swamps and marshes and rivers and the Everglades and, when all those reservoirs are filled, in huge underground aquifers. Nature's engineering work—the placing of rock strata to channel the water, the careful tilting of strata to move the water slowly, and the insertion of underground dams to block salt water intrusion—is of such skill and delicacy as to make the mighty Corps of Engineers resemble small boys dabbling in mud. Almost none of the rain that falls on Florida is allowed to escape quickly. When the white man first came to North America, Florida's resources of fresh water were as unmeasurable as the flocks of passenger pigeons that roofed eastern skies and the herds of bison that shook the plains.

The state is a true creature of the water, both fresh and salt. It has 1,300 miles of major coastline and 7,700 miles of secondary tidal coastline, more than any other state but Alaska. No part of the land is more than sixty miles from tidewater. A recent Florida atlas solemnly pointed out that if the continental shelf around the peninsula lifted only five hundred feet, the area of the state would be doubled. It is perhaps more intriguing to ask what might happen if the sea level instead of the land were raised. A rise of only twenty feet would submerge nearly every coastal community and the whole southern end of the state. A hundred-foot flood would leave nothing but smallish islands. If

At Sunken Gardens in St. Petersburg
a flock of pink flamingos clusters around a pond.

Florida people: *right*, a girls' chorus; *opposite*, a folksinger and a lasso twirler, all performing at the annual White Springs Folk Festival on the Suwanee River.

the water climbed 345 feet above present sea level, only Edward Bok's Singing Tower at Lake Wales would remain, hovering like a fairytale lighthouse over reefs that once were Florida. This is not at all fanciful. Florida has been under the sea before and, like Atlantis, will slip under again, whenever the polar ice caps weep a few extra tears into the Seven Seas.

The typewriter of the press agent has tapped out countless words in praise of Florida's weather, and almost none of them have been exaggerated. For six months a year, from November through April, a parade of blue-gold days dances across the calendar. This is the dry season, and rain usually comes only when a cold front trundles down from the continental mass. Tallahassee in the northern Panhandle averages only nineteen days a winter when the temperature edges below freezing. Miami has one such day and Key West none. As May comes, a subtle change takes place. Continental air loses its power to influence Florida weather, and sea breezes and trade winds move in. Big shiny clouds balloon through the sky. Most of them are caused by rising thermal currents as the land heats more quickly than the water. The most spectacular demonstration of this is in the Florida Keys where, on calm summer mornings, a pearl of cumulus forms above each parent island and joins an aerial necklace that follows the entire line of keys. In time such clouds may darken into thunderheads with secret passageways where lightning wanders, or they may breed purple line squalls.

In the northern United States, rain can be gentle or dreary. In Florida, summer rain is often sudden and dramatic, its coming marked by the kettledrum overtures of thunder and its ending by the hallelujah chorus of frogs. Summer is also the hurricane season, when whirlpools of air suck up heat from tropic waters and use it to fuel energy cells a hundred miles wide and ten miles high. Most parts of Florida have about one chance in ten of a hurricane in any given year. Scientists have been experimenting with the control of hurricanes through cloud seeding, working cautiously and even a bit fearfully, like junior sorcerers making their first try at summoning up the devil. No solid results have emerged from this program.

Indians discovered the advantages of living in Florida many thousands of years ago. The earliest Indians may have hunted elephants and bisons; when these animals became extinct Floridians had to satisfy themselves with lesser game—possums, raccoons, deer and turkeys, and with shellfish which have always been a staple of the Florida diet. Huge quantities of shellfish were eaten—mussels and clams and oysters and conchs; the shells were often fashioned into tools which could hollow out dugout canoes. Sometime after 1000 B.C., the Indians began to cultivate the soil. Once agriculture took hold, the population increased greatly and Indians expanded into previously uninhabited areas, such as the Everglades. In this period, Indians buried their dead—and sometimes dogs and alligators as well—in huge burial mounds. They traded extensively, reaching as far north as the Ohio Valley and all along the Gulf Coast. In various parts of Florida there were sizable Indian villages, built on top of shell mounds, containing temples and plazas where religious ceremonies took place.

To Ponce de Leon these Indians must have been a great disappointment. They had no precious metals and their land was not worth colonizing and their reaction to the sight of a Spaniard was to try to kill him. Ponce de Leon was not, by the way, seeking a Fountain of Youth, but merely trying to prove that there was a lot of youth left in his fifty-year-old body, an urge that many subsequent visitors to Florida have also felt. Not until years after the voyages of Ponce de Leon did the Fountain of Youth legend appear in any records. We do not know just where he made his first landfall. It may have been in the area of Cape Kennedy: Spanish swords and banners lifting toward heaven where now the Apollo rocket probes the sky. His final landfall, on his second voyage, is also a matter of dispute, but Charlotte Harbor on the west coast has the best claim. As usual the Indians were unfriendly. One of their arrows found a chink in expensive armor, and so Florida, in exchange for its lovely name, gave Ponce de Leon his death.

Blood and wounds never discouraged the conquistadores, however, and other captains came. They were unbelievable men. The soldiers of the Narvaez and De Soto expeditions marched in

Florida plants: *Above, left to right,* oranges, water hyacinth, poinsettia; *opposite,* water lilies at Ocheesee Pond in northwest Florida.

brutal damp heat. Mosquitoes thickened the air they breathed and redbugs burrowed into their flesh and thorns clawed at them and Indians waited with ugly shell-tipped arrows. No doubt these unbelievable men would have marched through every square mile of Florida had it been worth their while. What stopped them was not hardship but lack of reward. As time went on, the Spaniards left most of Florida untouched, and concentrated on building a chain of forts and missions across the north from St. Augustine to Pensacola.

For three hundred years after the voyages of Ponce de Leon a great many haphazard and untidy events came to pass. Florida had no real value to Spain and France and England except as a buffer area, but each feared that one of the others might get some great and secret advantage from the place. So they fought over Florida like dogs contesting for a dry and marrowless bone. They raided each other's settlements and carried out nasty little slaughters. Eventually they began trading Florida back and forth. Spain swapped it to England for Havana in 1763. England swapped it back, in 1783, in exchange for the Bahamas and Gibraltar. Pressure on Florida from the new United States began rising, and eventually Spain shrugged and gave up her profitless colony in 1821.

During these hollow centuries one major change was taking place. The native Indian tribes—the Pensacola, Timucua, Calusa, Mayaimi, Matacumbe and others—vanished. They were wiped out by the diseases of the white man, the softening effect of mission life in northern Florida, and raids by the Creek tribes of Georgia. The only Indians left were newcomers, the Creeks, who moved slowly down into the peninsula in front of the push of white settlers. Their numbers were swelled by escaped slaves, and the new tribe became known as Seminoles: the Wild Ones or Runaways. The whites, of course, were never in favor of Indians holding desirable land or harboring escaped slaves. The usual dreary Indian wars began. They followed the classic pattern of white pressure for land, Indian unrest, treaties by which the Indians sought peace by giving up some land, more pressure by settlers, Indian raids, army campaigns in which the wiping out of any Indian village was a victory and any loss was called a massacre, resettlement of Indians elsewhere, treacherous capture of Indian leaders (Osceola), and so on and so on. But there was one difference. After the Indians had been defeated and shipped off to Oklahoma, it turned out that some of them were still in Florida and willing to go on fighting. They retreated to such harsh areas as the

Florida people: *right*, retirees at a senior citizens' center in St. Petersburg; *opposite*, a Cuban sandwich-maker in Tampa; a cigar-maker in Key West.

Devil's Garden and Big Cypress and the Everglades, and dared the army to come after them. Nobody wanted to do this. The Seminoles were now occupying useless land and it was convenient to forget them.

It was no accident that the start of the Second Seminole War in 1835 coincided with a major freeze. Citrus groves had been developed along the St. John's River in the northeast. This was an event of great importance; for the first time Florida had a real money crop that was safe from competition. Oranges matured in cool weather and could be shipped with little risk of spoilage. But in 1835 came a bad freeze. It damaged the St. John's groves and sent people farther south—Indians or no Indians—seeking land more protected from frost. From 1835 to the present, the southward migration in Florida has often been spurred by freezes.

Florida became a state in 1845. When the Civil War came the population was 140,000, of which about half was Negro. Since many of the settlers had come from Georgia, and there were quite a few plantations using slave labor to grow cotton and sugar cane, it was inevitable that the state would join the Confederacy. What seems curious, however, is that Florida was so enthusiastic about it. Florida was the third state to secede, and 15,000 men out of a total white population of 70,000 enlisted. Five thousand paid the final price for their enthusiasm. During the war Florida was a backwater area with Union forces holding some key points on the coasts, and Confederates holding the interior. There were only two engagements classed as battles, neither of importance except to the men who happened to get killed in them. Florida's real value to the Confederacy was as a supplier of beef and hides and pork and tobacco and salt.

Most wars shake up patterns of living and create restless movements of people. The Reconstruction period ended late in Florida but, by 1876, people began moving into the state in greater and greater numbers. These were not the tourists of modern days. They were farmers, ex-soldiers, artisans from northern cities, immigrants from Europe—all looking for cheap land, of which there was plenty. Another migration also started from the south. Key West had had a cigar industry since 1831, importing tobacco and workers from Cuba. Now the first of a series of revolutions hit Cuba, and refugees began coming to Florida. These troubles pro-

duced something of a bonanza for the Florida cattle barons, who found that the Spanish Army in Cuba would pay gold for the scrawny cattle of Florida's thin pastures. It seems ironic that the Spaniards, who searched so hard for gold in Florida, ended by shipping it there.

In 1881 Florida found another source of gold, this time a vein that is still being mined. The source was the tourist with money to invest. The visitor in this case was Horace Disston, a Philadelphia saw manufacturer, and the sum of money was one million dollars. Florida officials coaxed Disston to pay that for 4,000,000 acres of swampland in the general area of Lake Okeechobee. The state had good reasons for the sale: debts that had almost ruined its credit. Disston's reasons for buying are not so evident. One might claim that, to a shrewd Philadelphian, land at twenty-five cents an acre would be an irresistible bargain. But a shrewd Philadelphian might also wonder what was wrong with such cheap land. Was Disston shrewd or not? We do not know. This may have been another case in which Florida's golden air bemused a practical man and entangled him in visions.

Disston bought two dredges and sent them up the Caloosahatchee to drain his 4,000,000 acres. It is symbolic that Florida's first big-scale land developer relied on the dredge, which was to become the essential tool as well as the curse of Florida. The state, with its boundless flat watery land, is peculiarly suited to dredge operations. A dredge can be turned loose in wet land and go on indefinitely, digging its own private waterway and piling up the spoil on both sides. Even today, far down in the wildness of Everglades National Park between Flamingo and Cape Sable, one can find such channels knifing off into the distance, unused, unneeded, untended, dating back a half century or more. It is tempting to listen in the silence for a ghostly clanking and to wonder if a phantom crew is still at work. Disston did not succeed in draining his 4,000,000 acres or in creating the canal-laced empire that he had planned. He must, however, have had a remarkably exciting time spending his money, and he was followed by two men who brought in even larger sums of money and operated on an even bigger scale and, no doubt, were just as entangled by visions. They were Henry M. Flagler and Henry B. Plant, and they bedecked Florida with railroads like a man courting a woman with jewels.

Like other states, Florida had passed laws grant-

ing public lands to railroad builders. In most cases the lands had to be certified as "swamp and overflowed." This led to the use of such devices as putting a boat in a wagon and carting it over good dry land, in order to certify that the land could only be traversed by boat. It was also possible to send a construction crew with a half-mile of track and one steam engine out into the palmetto country, laying track ahead of the engine and tearing it up behind, in order to claim the land grants for laying hundreds of miles of track. These shell-game exploits had produced many tiny railroads whose promoters grabbed their profits and vanished, leaving debts and parallel streaks of rust.

Flagler and Plant were men of a different breed. Both were rich, Flagler from working with Rockefeller in Standard Oil, and Plant from ownership of Southern Express Company. They began buying the bankrupt railroad companies, and started an epic contest with each other that could only have happened in the age of laissez-faire capitalism. Flagler pushed his steel down the east coast while Plant netted central Florida and the west coast with his lines. Neither of them, apparently, wasted much time thinking about who would ride on these endless rails and what freight would be shipped on them. They were empire builders moving amid golden visions, and such men do not take inventory like shopkeepers. Now and then they did realize that not enough people were riding their trains, and at such times they built magnificent hotels—the Ponce de Leon in St. Augustine, and the Tampa Bay Hotel with its dreamlike domes and minarets—to coax people to come to Florida. Flagler's final vision was of a railroad spanning the seas in a steel rainbow from Biscayne Bay to Key West. Naturally, he built it despite fantastic engineering problems.

In spite of Disston and Flagler and Plant, Florida was still in many ways a raw frontier as the twentieth century opened. At a time when the American West had been tamed, Florida was still resisting the crunch of civilization. It was a strange and tough and proud country, if one can apply the word proud to a piece of geography. In 1900 it still had its undefeated Indian tribe and its trackless wilderness and a host of surprises that it was waiting to unleash on newcomers. But it did have sun and huge open spaces and opportunity, and as the new century began, waves of people began coming in. They would increase Florida's population twelve times from 1900 up to the present.

Florida animals: *Left*, pelicans scrambling for fish at Islamorada. *Opposite, left to right*, a loggerhead turtle at Fort Walton Beach; raccoons in the Florida Panhandle; an elephant performing at the Circus Hall of Fame in Sarasota.

The slogan of the new century was "Drain the Everglades!" Nobody asked what effect this might have on the water supply and the weather and the land itself, because these were not questions that people had learned to ask. When something stood in the way of progress, like too much water, one removed it. A new governor with a ringing name, Napoleon Broward, led the assault. Dredges and draglines swarmed out through the land, chewing through the sawgrass and mangrove like enormous locusts. Up around Lake Okeechobee, the farmers rejoiced in deep muck soil, now dry enough to farm. Only a few of them thought it odd that the land kept sinking around their houses by a foot each year. Nobody had ever heard of land that would actually oxidize and vanish. The draining of the Everglades and other areas went on.

Another war came along (it was called, with the charming naïveté of those times, the "War to End Wars") and sent another restless migration of people into Florida. This wave produced a phenomenon that has been referred to ever since in capital letters: the Florida Boom. There had been land gambles before in the state but always on a relatively small scale. The Florida Boom was on the gigantic scale of the South Sea Bubble and the Dutch Tulip Craze and the Mississippi Bubble; once it got started, it drew in people and money as automatically as a magnet collects iron filings. Nobody paused to ask if corner lots were really worth thousands of dollars a front foot or if land beyond city limits could ever repay an investment of $30,000 an acre.

A favorite story concerned a newcomer who arrived in Miami and met an old friend. The friend asked jokingly if he had made any money yet. The newcomer cried, "I certainly did! I had no more than got off the train when a guy hurried up to me and bought my dog for ten thousand dollars!" The friend said, "Good heavens, he paid ten thousand in cash?" The newcomer said, "Well, not exactly, but he gave me a pair of five thousand dollar cats."

All over Florida, people accepted pairs of five thousand dollar cats for their ten thousand dollar dogs. And yet this was not at all a deliberate flimflam, a racket, a confidence game. People believed in Florida and the Boom as they believed in Motherhood and the American Dream. And there were at least a dozen empire builders who had been caught by golden visions. John Collins and Carl F. Fisher were creating the dreamland of Miami Beach. Joseph W. Young spent millions filling

Florida's economy: *left to right,* a shrimp boat, Fernandina Beach; calico scallops—along with a lone starfish—at Fort Pierce; trucks unloading oranges; phosphate piled for storage before shipping.

swamps in the Fort Lauderdale area, planning a modern Venice. George Merrick plotted the new city of Coral Gables in which everything was foreseen and controlled right up to the color of the tiles on the Spanish-type roofs. On the west coast, D. P. Davis pumped up eight hundred acres of magnificent islands from the bottom of Tampa Bay. Farther south, Barron G. Collier went empire-building with his streetcar advertising millions, buying kingly slices of land and coaxing the legislature to confirm his royal rights by letting him form his own private Collier County. Everywhere in the state the big and medium-sized and little promoter staked out raw land and gave it poetic names and sold it.

The whole thing, of course, was simply a financial game of musical chairs, except that nobody realized fate might start removing chairs. The first chair vanished when an old ship, under tow with a load of lumber for Miami's builders, broke loose and blocked the ship channel for months. The next chair vanished when the railroads, unable to keep up with freight shipments, put an embargo on the area. The third chair blew away. Few people had any idea what hurricanes could do, and nobody paid much heed to the odd breathless quality in the air of mid-September of 1926. The hurricane hit Miami and the Gold Coast at night. The next morning people hurried out in a sunny airless calm to see what the storm had done. Old-timers could have told them that this was suicidal. The hurricane had not passed; it was merely the calm center that had arrived. The screaming winds came back and people died by the hundreds; flimsy buildings took off like kites, and the Florida Boom left at the jet speed of a major hurricane.

It is easy now, many years later, to talk loftily of human greed and stupidity. But there cannot be real greed where people have dreams, and in the Florida Boom countless thousands of people were caught up by the idea that they were aiding in the birth of a promised land, an Eden, an earthly paradise. Nor can people be accused of stupidity when they have no way of learning; they may be ignorant, but not stupid. One of the odd results of the Florida Boom was that almost no one escaped from it with a fortune. Most of the great developers went bankrupt. Paper profits vanished. The boom-time streets marched emptily out into the palmetto country, sinking lower each year into undergrowth. There were, however, solid additions to Florida's wealth. The boom may have gone, but the new Miami Beach and Coral Gables and the Davis Islands and a hundred other creations remained . . . along with the giant half-completed Miami hotel that, in the 1930's, became a home for 60,000 laying hens and 20,000 fryers.

Florida went through a convalescent period in the Depression, and then got a transfusion of health from the training camps of World War II.

Afterward another postwar migration started. This was different from those that followed the Civil War and World War I, because many of the people who came from the north were not seeking their fortunes but only a better way of living. It was a migration fueled by Social Security checks and private pension plans and early retirement and savings produced by the Affluent Society. As it came, towns swelled into cities. The shiny igloos of mobile homes popped out by the scores of thousands, and new communities painted their checkerboard patterns on the land, and suddenly, almost shockingly, white cliffs rose along favorite beaches as hotels and condominiums and co-ops shouldered up from the wet sand. From Cuba came another migration, a flood of the dispossessed fleeing the steamroller flattening of Communism.

So, as the last quarter of the century neared, Florida was no longer an empty land seeking its destiny but the ninth state in population, trailing only California in number of people gained between 1960 and 1970. It is appropriate, therefore, to ask whether or not what has happened is good, and to what extent, and if what will happen in the future will be better or worse.

Florida is still an improbably big and varied land. From Pensacola to Key West the road distance is 805 miles, as far as from New York City to Chicago. Within this great curvature of land can be found the red clay and slow black rivers of the north, the central highlands lacquered green with a million acres of citrus, and the River of Grass—the Everglades—unique in all the world. The white sands of St. Augustine and Daytona, the coralline strands of the Gold Coast, and the powdery shell beaches of the Gulf of Mexico are still in place. The great crystal fountains continue to spout at Silver Springs and Wakulla and Homosassa and Weekiwachee. The Ten Thousand Islands remain untouched, a green jigsaw puzzle that nature built and then joggled slightly, so that each piece drew a bit away from the next. There is yet one realm of virgin cypress, Corkscrew Swamp, a place of strange and awesome beauty, a watery cathedral columned by the big trees. The Florida Keys carve their scimitar way through turquoise and amethyst and emerald and sapphire waters, and the tarpon still leap, creatures of molten silver, in the moonlight. Then, too, there remain the sea and the clouds and wind, and the sun, the sun, the sun.

All these are bequests from nature, and man can only take credit for not having yet destroyed them. But there are also man-made things of note. The state is anchored in the sea by two unbelievable forts. In the northeast, at St. Augustine, is the fort that everybody visits: the Castillo de San Marcos, of which a Spanish king said querulously, "They must be building it out of solid silver." To the southwest, beyond the reach of road and where no motel flashes its neon offer, lies the fort that almost nobody visits: Fort Jefferson of the Dry Tortugas, which was to have been the Gibraltar of the Caribbean but which never fired a gun in anger. The Spanish king was not so badly off as he thought, paying $30,000,000 to build the Castillo de San Marcos. Fort Jefferson has 40,000,000 bricks in its walls, and each brick is said to have cost a dollar for transportation alone.

Between these two fantasies lie the cities and resorts that man has built and which, sleazy or monumental, ugly or beautiful, have yet provided a better life to a host of people than they had elsewhere. Florida has never had a problem of emigration; those who come to the state to live seldom leave it willingly. Florida is still a land of magic where myths and legends fatten like Valencia oranges. If you do not believe in Florida magic you should not visit Cape Kennedy, where man rides an ultimate flame into black space, nor should you go to Disney World, where one can ride imagination back into the delights of childhood.

Whether or not this way of life can continue, and offer a haven to the millions who may want to come to Florida in the future, depends on man's skill in solving the enormous problems he has brought to the state. Until recently, nobody thought about such things. A century ago it was great sport to ride a steamboat on a Florida river and shoot the huge alligators sunning on the banks. The plume hunters were more practical; they almost wiped out the egrets, but for profit. We read of Teddy Roosevelt, who launched the government on some of its early conservation projects, landing a harmless two-ton manta ray after his party shot almost fifty steel-jacketed bullets into it. We can almost see the bright gleam of his eyeglasses and hear his happy shout, "Bully!" He did not mean to be unsporting, any more than did the marksmen who potted alligators. They knew no better. They had no idea of the balance of nature and of how one creature depends on the next, and of how mankind depends on all of them.

The assaults on Florida's wildlife, however, have been minor compared to the assaults on the physical environment. Wildlife can recover under the right conditions. Certain things done to the environment may be irreversible. It is an odd fact that the two areas of the United States that proved most difficult for man to tame—Florida and Alaska—are perhaps the most fragile. Both are like fine crystal that resists change completely up to a certain point, and then shatters.

The greatest asset of Florida has been the huge quantity of fresh water that it receives and its natural and unique ability to retain that water. Men have been struggling for nearly a century to destroy this asset. Flood water gets in the way of farmers who prefer to irrigate their crops by pump. It drenches the lots of developers, and the roads that serve tourists. So men have worked feverishly to get rid of it. They are still trying to do so. Only one thing distinguishes Florida from the Sahara and Gobi and Mohave deserts. They are dry sandy areas. Florida is a wet sandy area.

Florida's problems are not the result of malice but of ignorance. It has been a difficult land to study and comprehend. The first farmers of the black Okeechobee muck could not understand why their vegetables grew magnificently and then suddenly split open. Nobody had analyzed the soil and proved that it was fantastically high in nitrogen but almost bare of many trace elements needed for growth. When billows of smoke began rising over the Everglades, thirty years ago, men could not believe that the very land was burning, all because it had been drained. The wells that now draw up salt instead of fresh water are a shock to many people. And who would dream that the porous soil cannot take care of the overflow from half a million septic tanks, or that the runoff from a pulp mill might kill life in a huge bay, or that a dam holding back phosphate sludge might break and cripple a river, or that a 120-square-mile lake named Apopka might die of fertilizer poisoning, or that the nation's only living coral reef, the Underwater State Park in the Keys, might begin to sicken from pollution and dredging?

These are some of the terrible problems that the fairytale land is facing. Perhaps it is improbable that men will, for once, be wise enough to pause and work out solutions and make possible a bright future. But Florida has always been an improbable land, and so perhaps . . . perhaps . . .

A Seminole woman sews the characteristically bright-colored Seminole fabric.

A HISTORICAL VIEW

Indians, Spaniards, the French, the English, Americans—Florida has seen a succession of masters. An early French visitor recorded the customs of the native Indians in a series of engravings. *Opposite top to bottom*, the Indians are shown setting an enemy village on fire, preparing a feast, and killing alligators. By the end of the eighteenth century the native Indians had died out, to be succeeded by the Seminoles, a branch of the Creek people. They, in turn, were for the most part driven out of Florida by the Americans in the 1830's, though Osceola, *above*, and other chiefs fought bitterly to keep their homes.

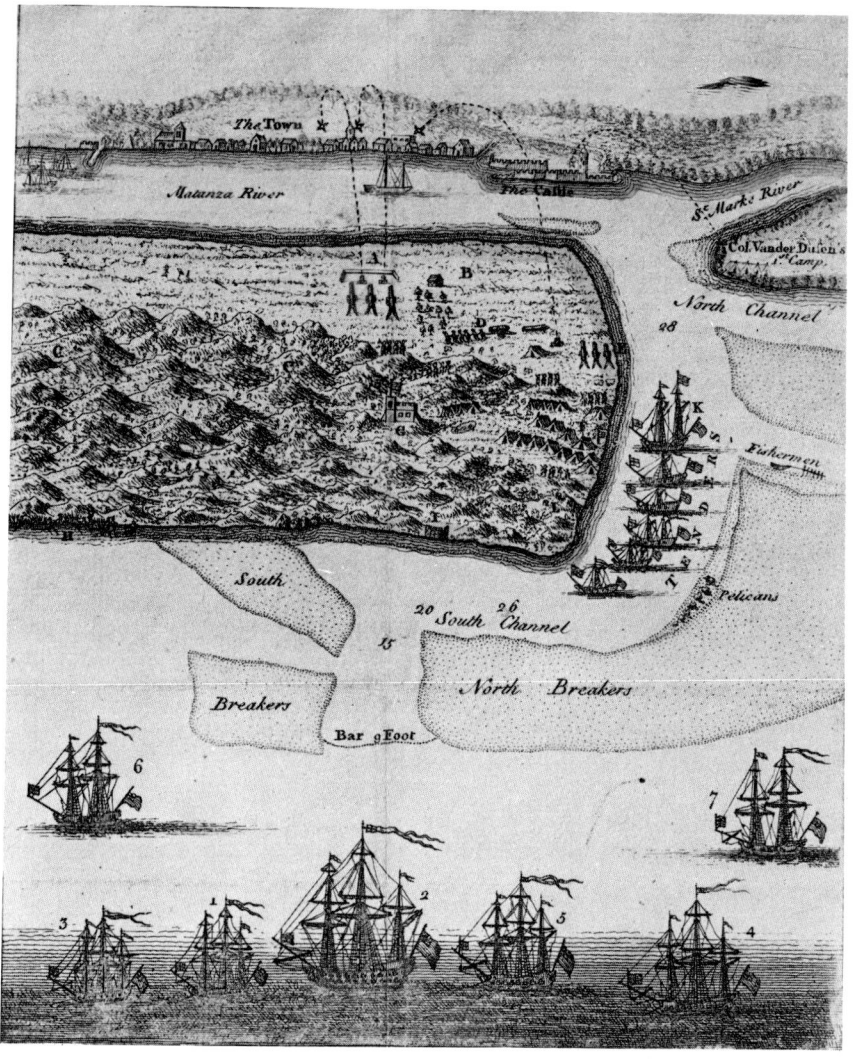

The Spaniards came to Florida in 1516, but it was not until 1559 that they established their first precarious settlement at Pensacola. St. Augustine, founded in 1565, was the first permanent settlement: *Opposite*, St. Augustine's Spanish-style La Leche chapel. In 1564 the French built a fort at the mouth of the St. John's River; a contemporary engraving, *upper left*, shows the fort's construction. The first appearance of the English in Florida was in 1586, when Sir Francis Drake sacked and burned St. Augustine. The next two centuries saw a three-cornered contest for control of the peninsula between France, England, and Spain, marked by numerous battles, including the 1740 English attack on St. Augustine shown at left. The contest remained unresolved until the beginning of the nineteenth century, when a new power—the United States—entered the scene.

Andrew Jackson fought against the Spaniards and the Seminoles, and became governor of Florida once Spain ceded the territory to the United States. The city of Jacksonville, named after him, was an early center of trade; *above*, a nineteenth-century engraving shows the busy waterfront. Another busy center, *shown right,* in an 1884 engraving, was Cedar Key, on the Gulf Coast, a center of turpentine manufacture.

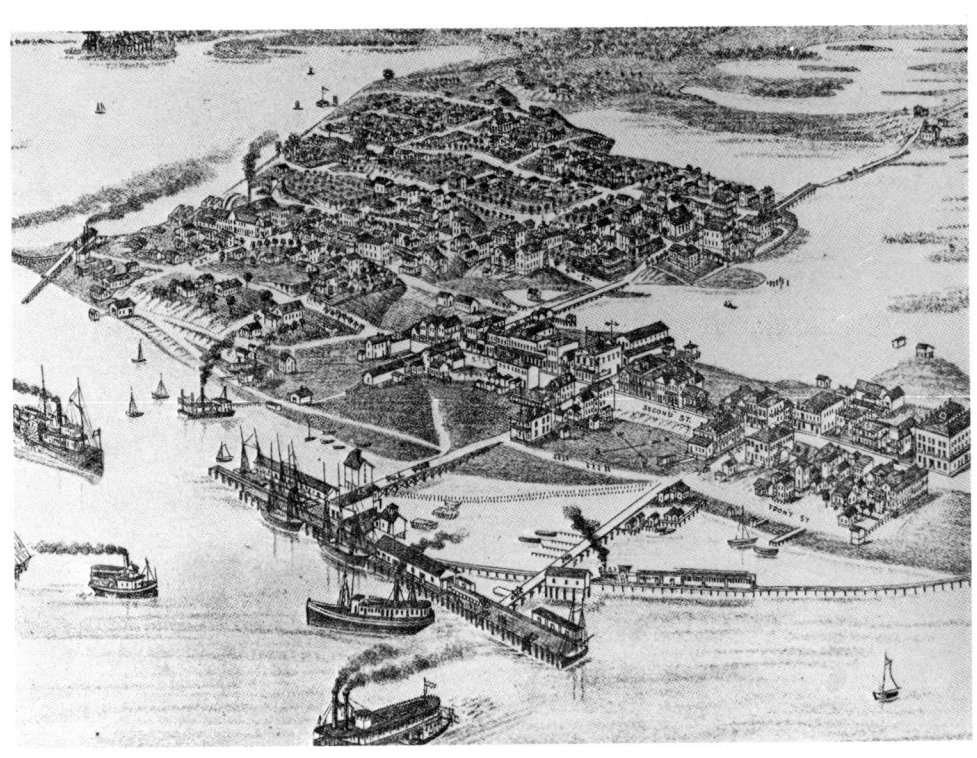

Throughout the nineteenth and early twentieth century Florida grew considerably, and its economy expanded and diversified. In the Civil War period cotton and turpentine were shipped out (an engraving, *above*, shows cotton being loaded on a train at New Fernandina). The Spanish first brought citrus fruit to Florida, but the expansion of cultivation took place only after the Civil War. Most years were productive and brought in new wealth, but occasionally—as seen *at left* in an 1895 picture—cold destroyed the crops. Tourism brought more growth to the state. At *upper left* is a 1923 land auction; *overleaf* are bathers disporting in the surf at Palm Beach.

A PICTURE TOUR

Twenty million tourists visit Florida each year, looking for the sun—going as far south toward the equator as they can in the United States. They loll on the beaches, bird-watch in the Everglades, boat along the state's miles of inland waterways, and watch a space capsule blast off for a tour of outer space. Here in miniature is a picture tour of the state they visit, covering more than 800 miles from one end of Florida to the other, beginning at the old town of Pensacola in the northwest and reaching to the Dry Tortugas in the far south. It is immensely varied, like the state it depicts; Florida's people, animals, plants, towns, monuments, and landscape are presented in pictures that evoke both the spirit and the unique beauty of the state whose very name means "flowery."

An aerial view of Pensacola shows the city's broad avenues sweeping down to Pensacola Bay. *Opposite,* the Old Cemetery in Pensacola.

Opposite, Pensacola's Fort San Carlos, first built in 1698. *At right and above*, characteristic wooden houses in Pensacola's five-block-long Historic District.

Above, at the small Gulf of Mexico fishing village of Destin, a fisherman unwinds net. *Opposite,* bright sunlight reddens dunes on Pensacola Beach.

Overleaf: At Destin, a long bridge spans East Pass, which connects the shallow waters of Choctawhatchee Bay with the Gulf of Mexico.

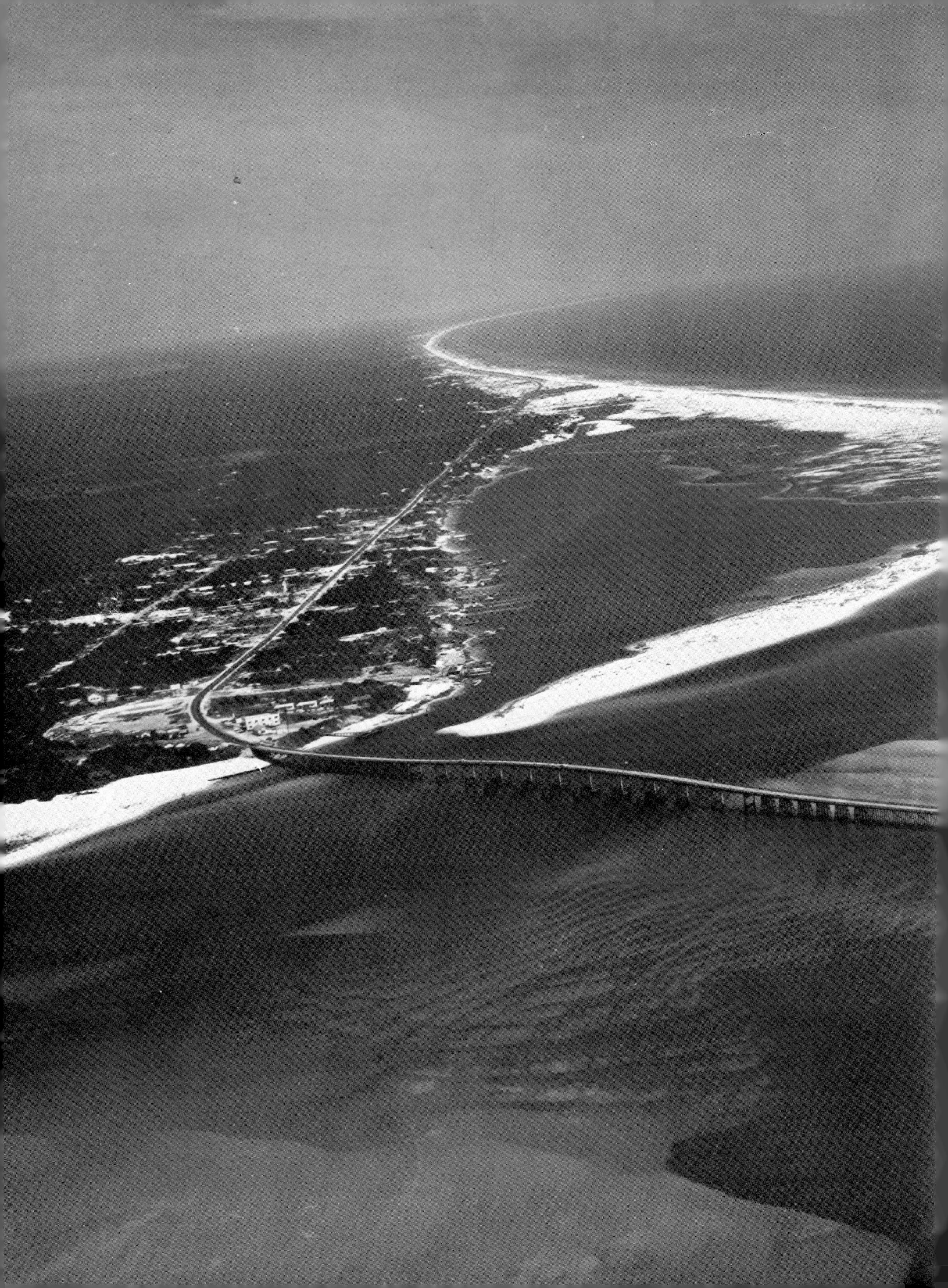

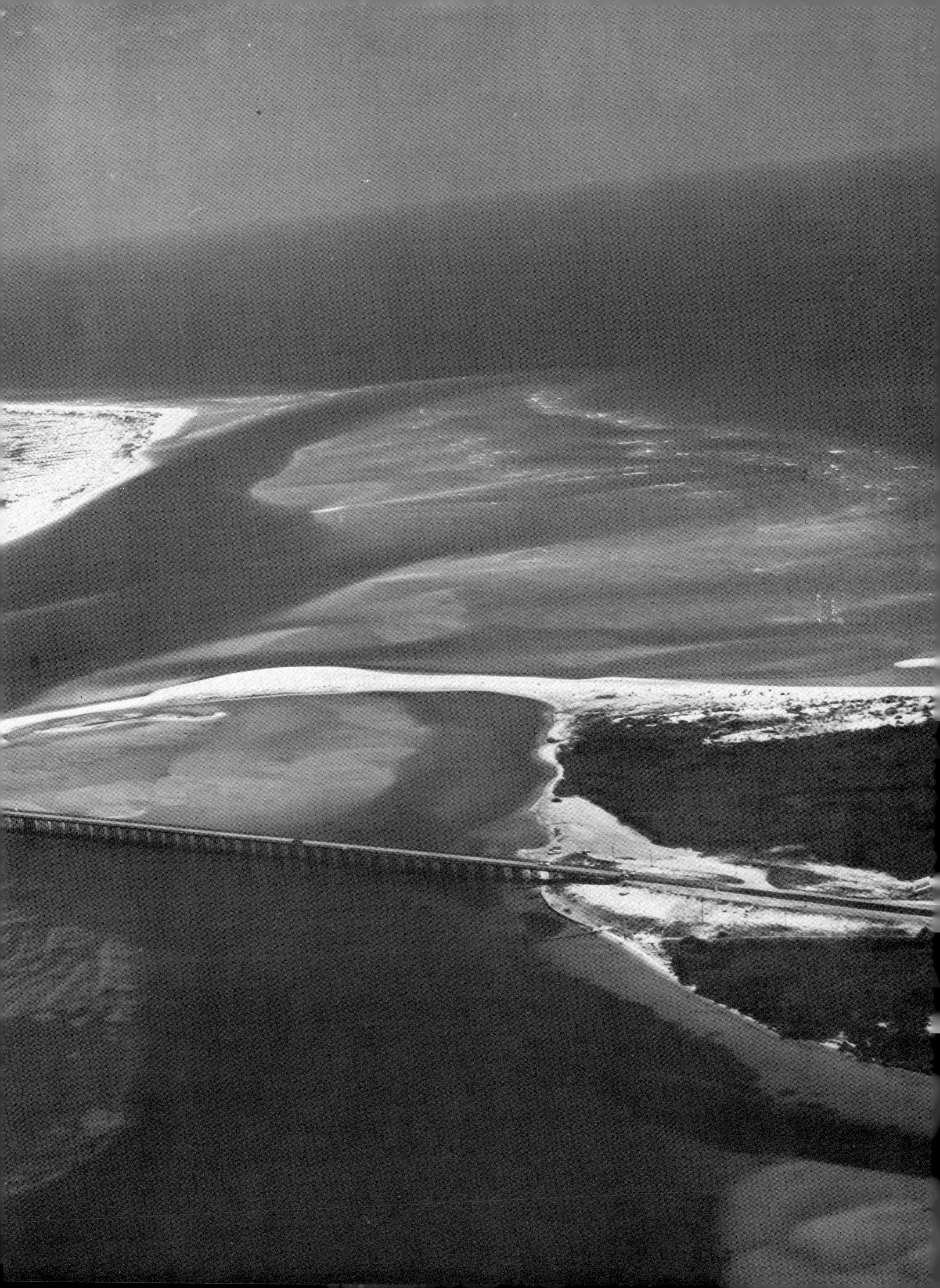

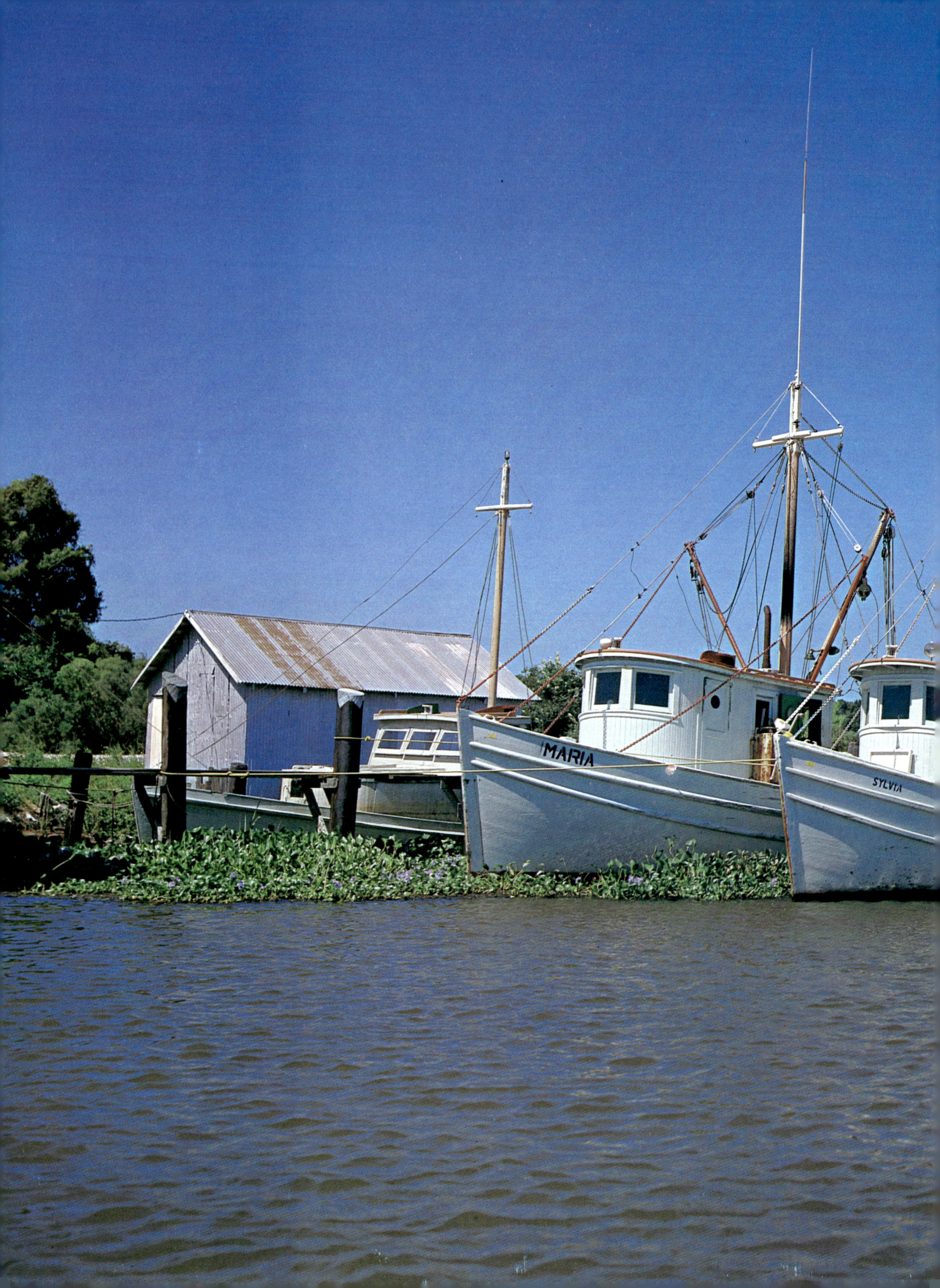
MARIA
SYLVIA

Three shrimp boats docked at Apalachicola.

The old town of Apalachicola, *opposite*, founded early in the nineteenth century, is a center of shellfisheries. The Valentine Hoffman house, *below*, dates from the 1840's. *At right* is the Baptist Church, a fine example of carpenter Gothic.

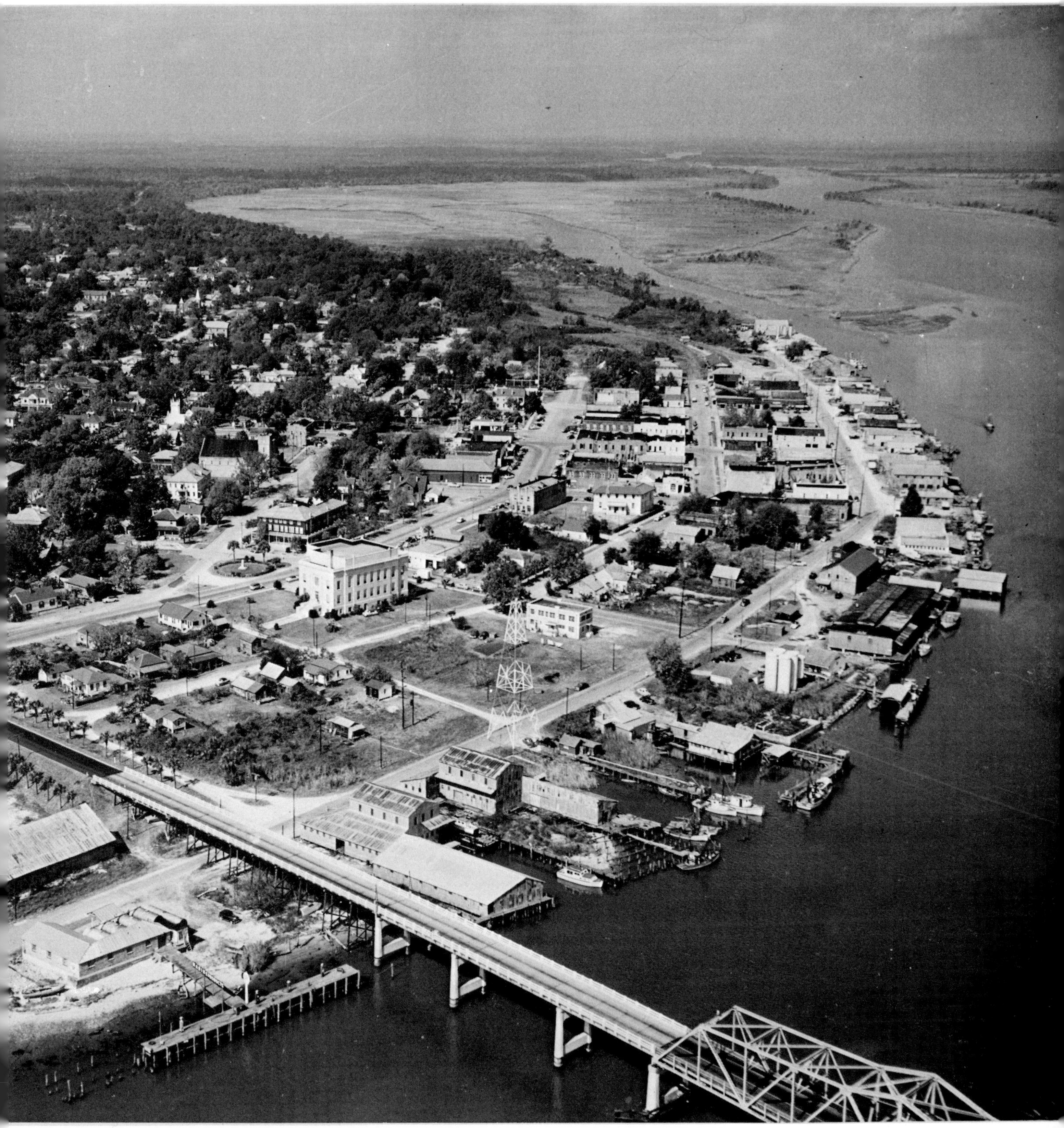

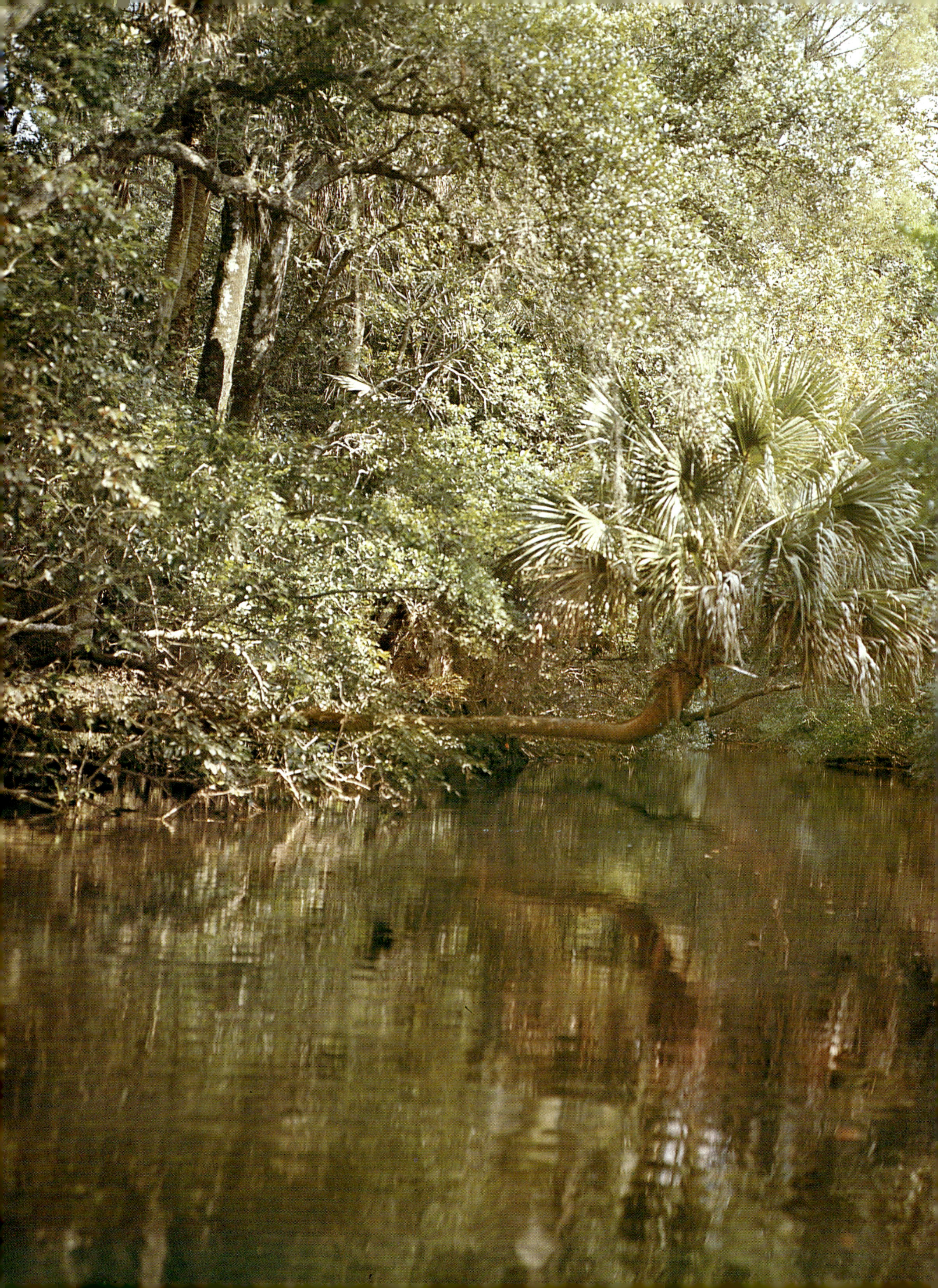

Left, the still waters of Juniper Spring Creek.
Below, the busy resort of Panama City.

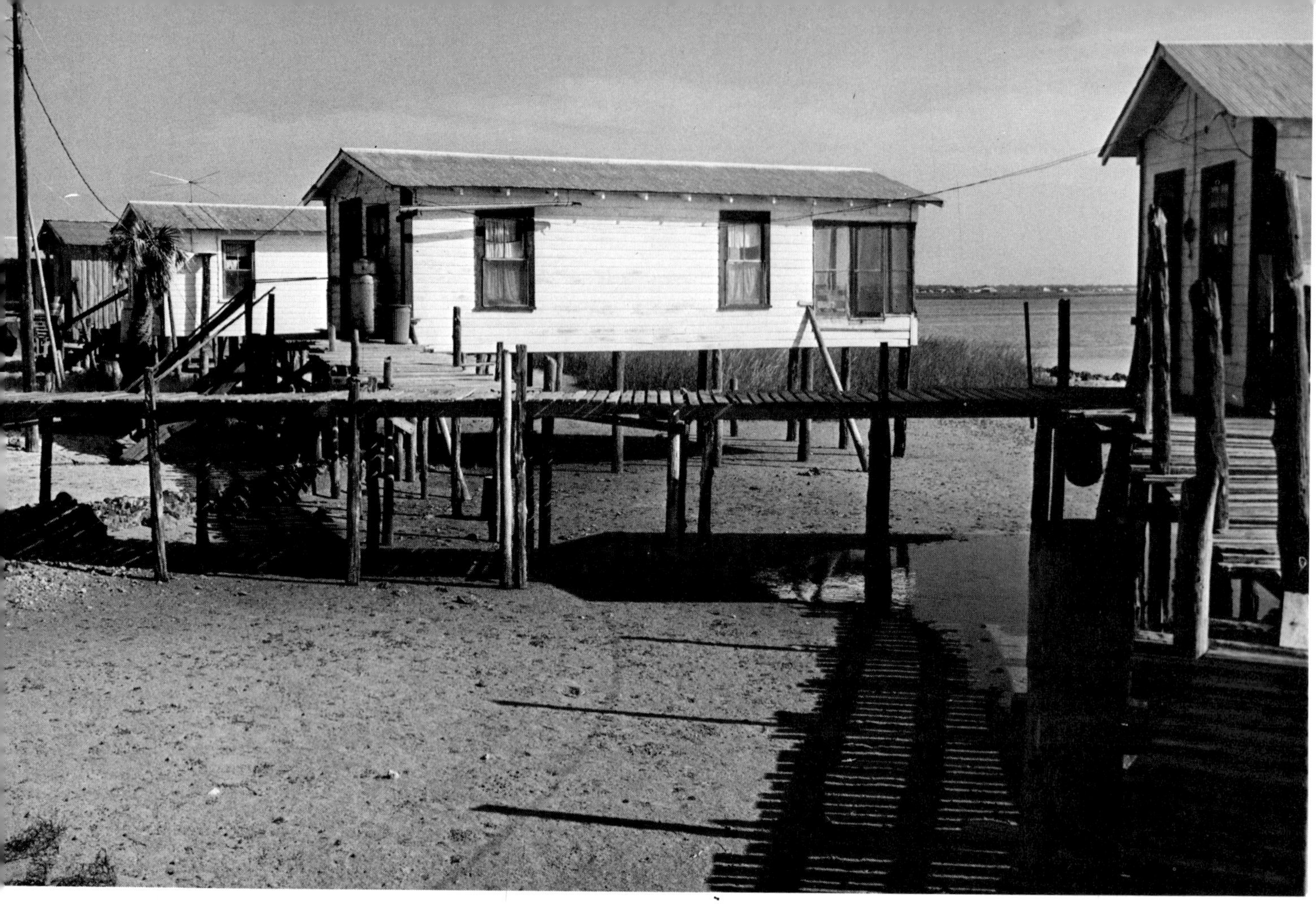

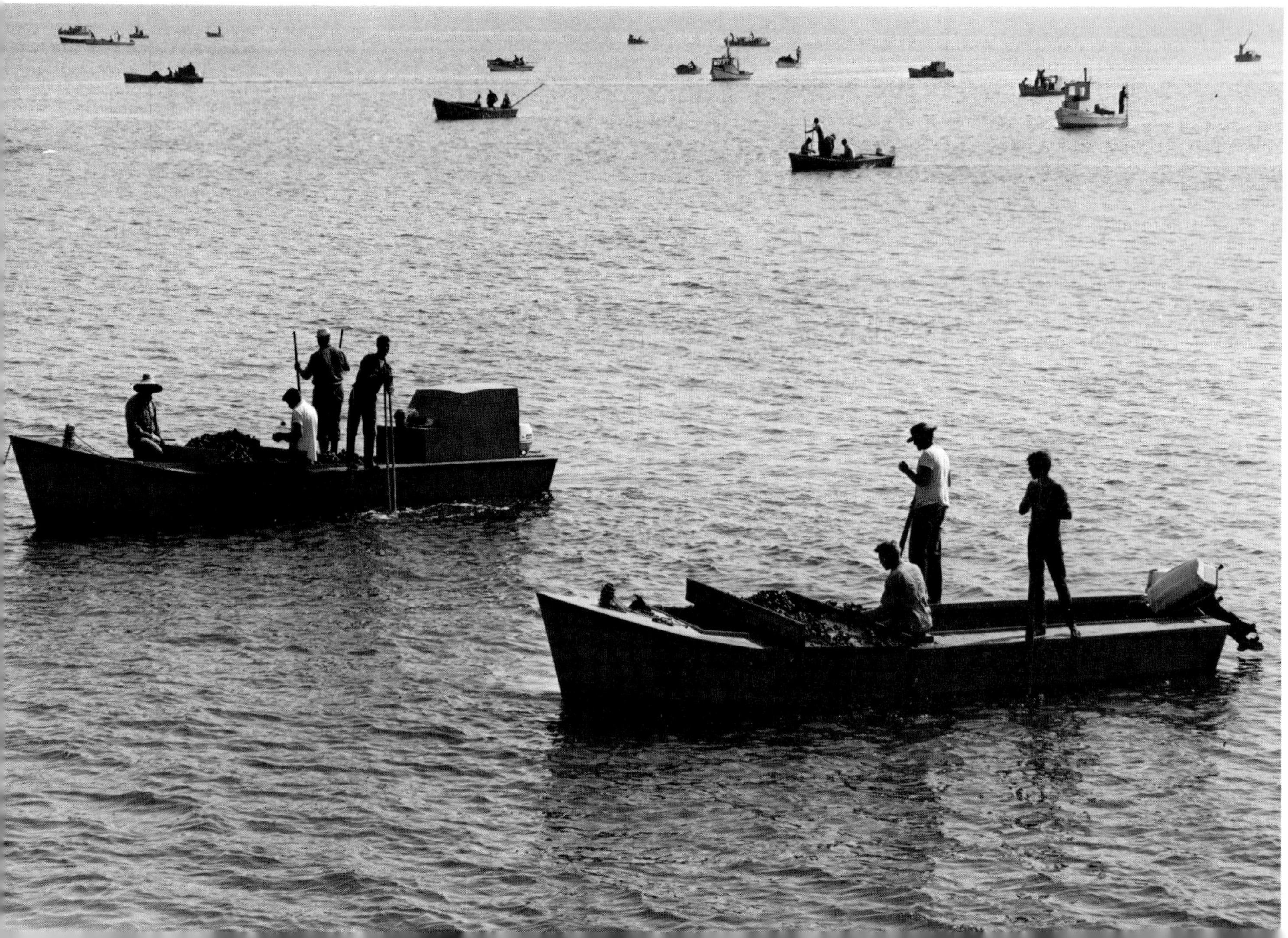

Above, an oval spring, which gives its name to the Panhandle town of De Funiak Springs. *Opposite, top,* beach houses on stilts, at Jug Island; *bottom,* the Apalachicola oyster fleet, which brings in nine-tenths of the state's catch.

Overleaf: At Florida Caverns State Park, northwest of Tallahassee, lies a network of beautifully colored caves, not discovered until 1937.

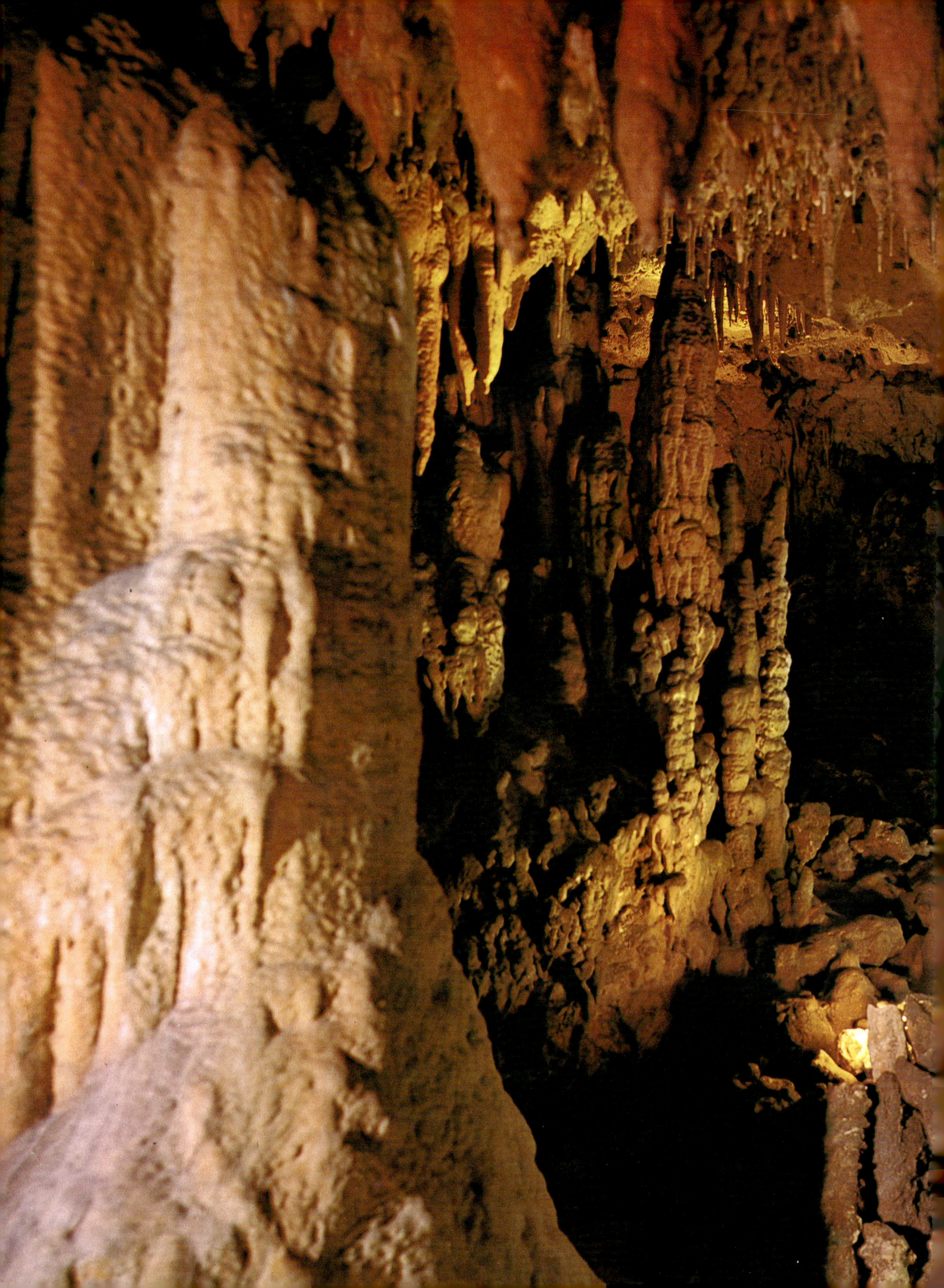

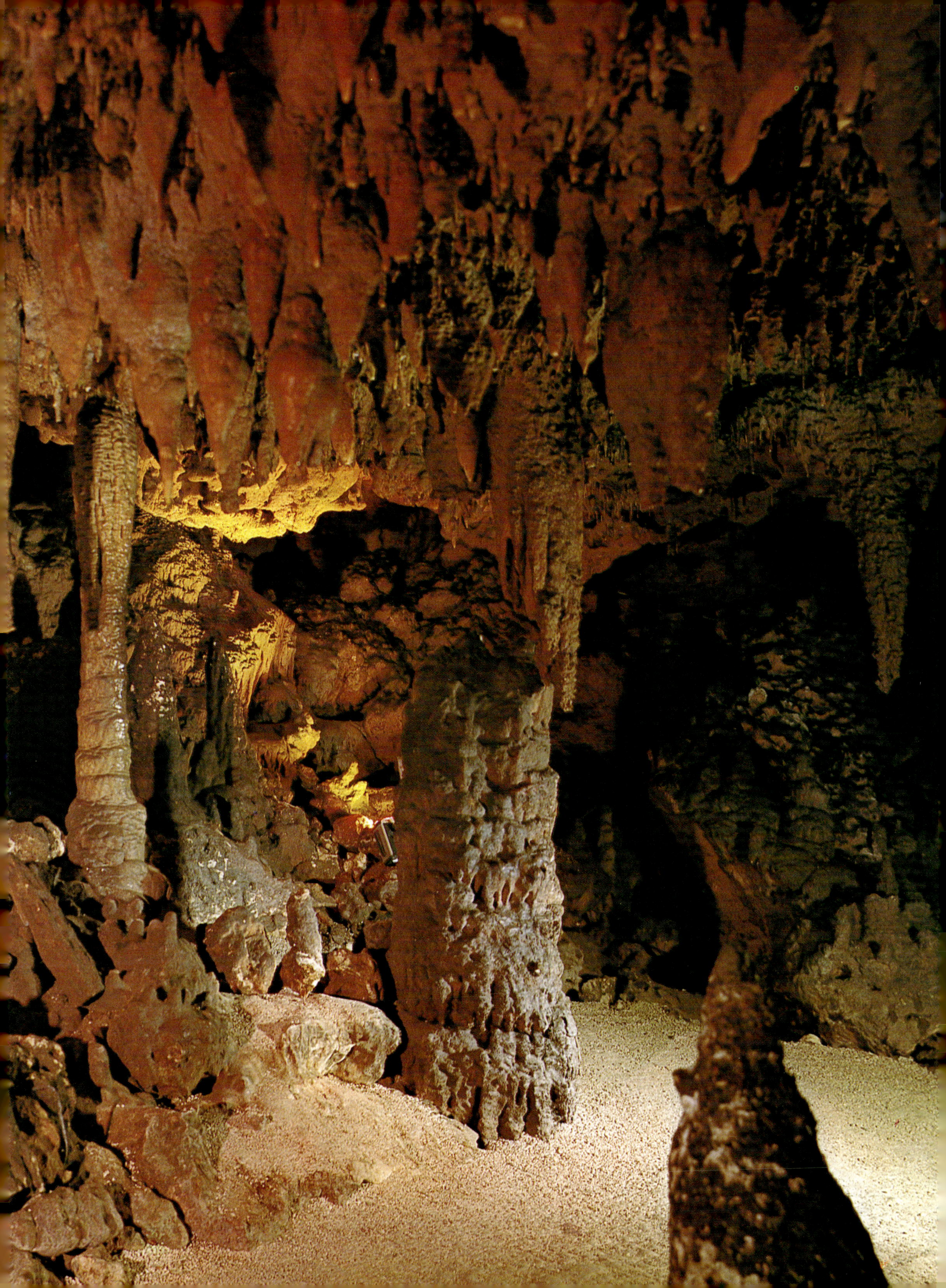

Old cannon guard the columned entrance to the state Capitol in Tallahassee, *opposite*. The symbols on the state seal—a cocoa palm, a steamboat, an Indian woman scattering flowers—decorate the pediment. *Below,* the Fine Arts Building at Florida State University in Tallahassee. *Left,* the tombs of Prince and Princess Murat (she was Washington's grandniece, he, Napoleon's nephew) outside the capital.

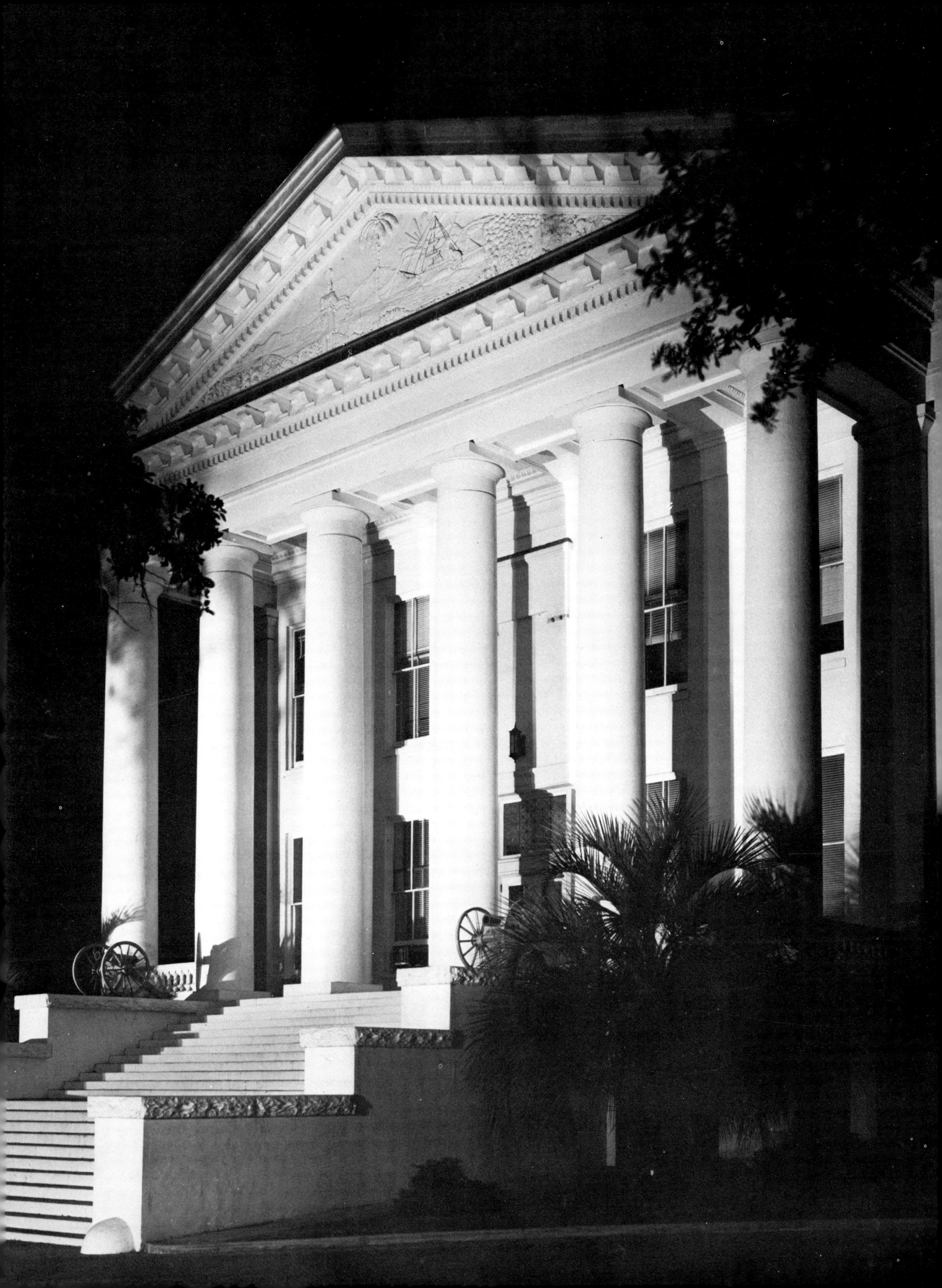

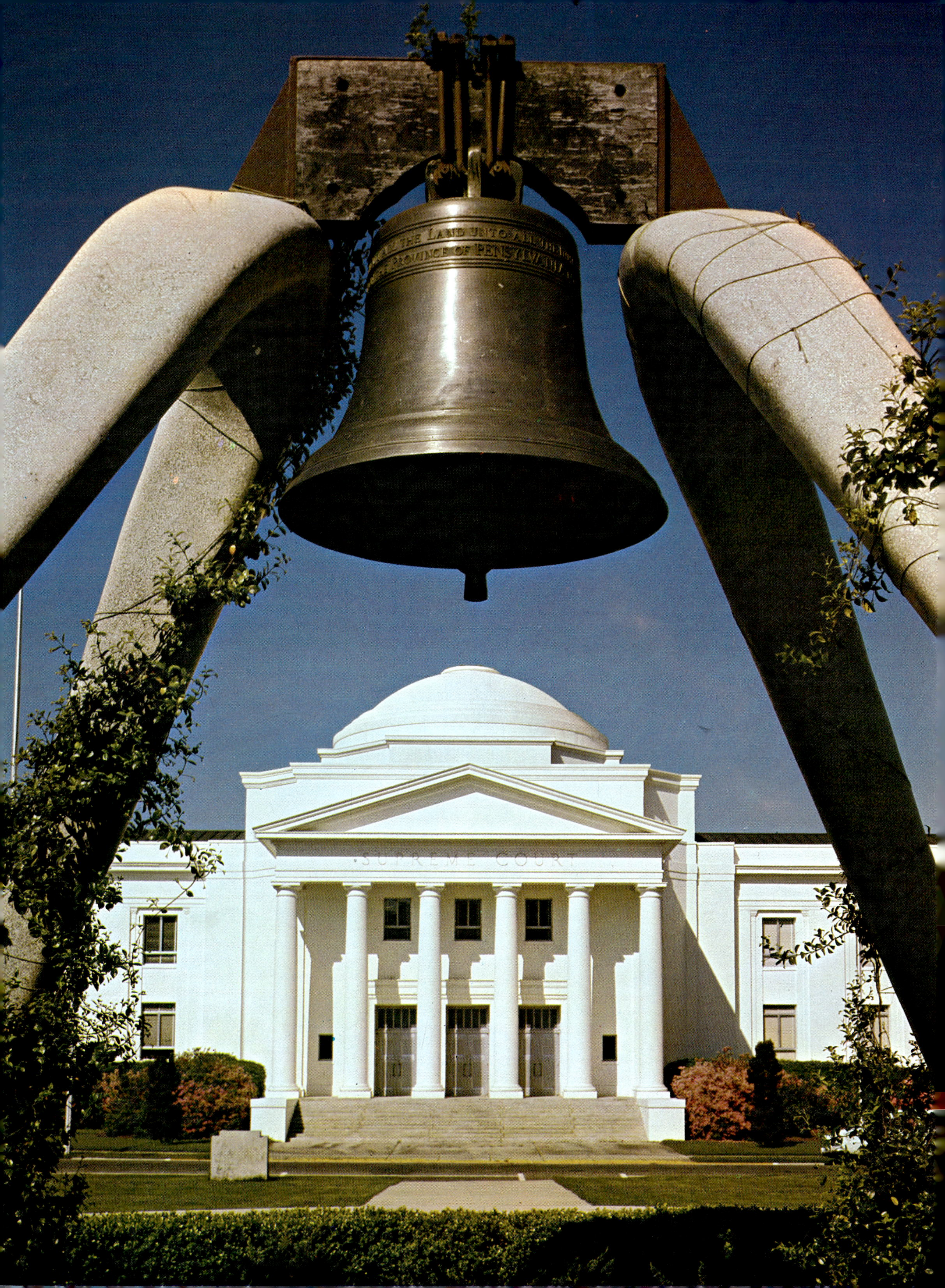
SUPREME COURT

Tallahassee is a city where flowers bloom year-round. *Above,* an old house surrounded by flowering trees and shrubs. *Opposite,* the classical State Supreme Court building, with a replica of the Liberty Bell in front of it.

The Panhandle region contains many old mansions. *At right*, the Eden mansion near Destin; *below*, the Gregory mansion near Bristol. The interior views, *opposite*, are from antebellum mansions near Tallahassee. *Top*, two views of "Goodwood"; *bottom*, a stair hall in "The Grove."

53

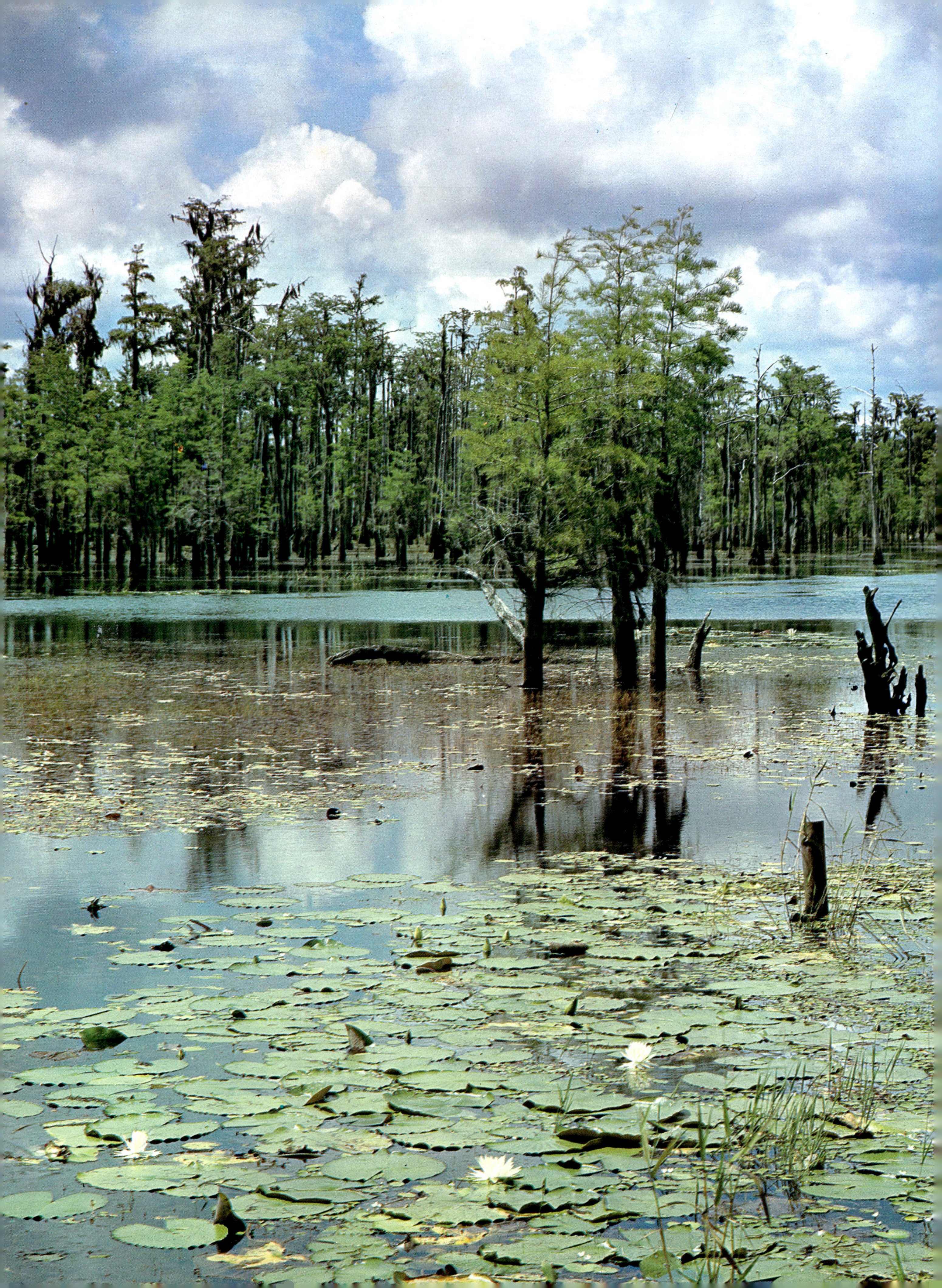

Above, a woodland stream near Newport.
Opposite, Ocheesee Pond, one of Florida's most beautiful and unspoiled ponds.

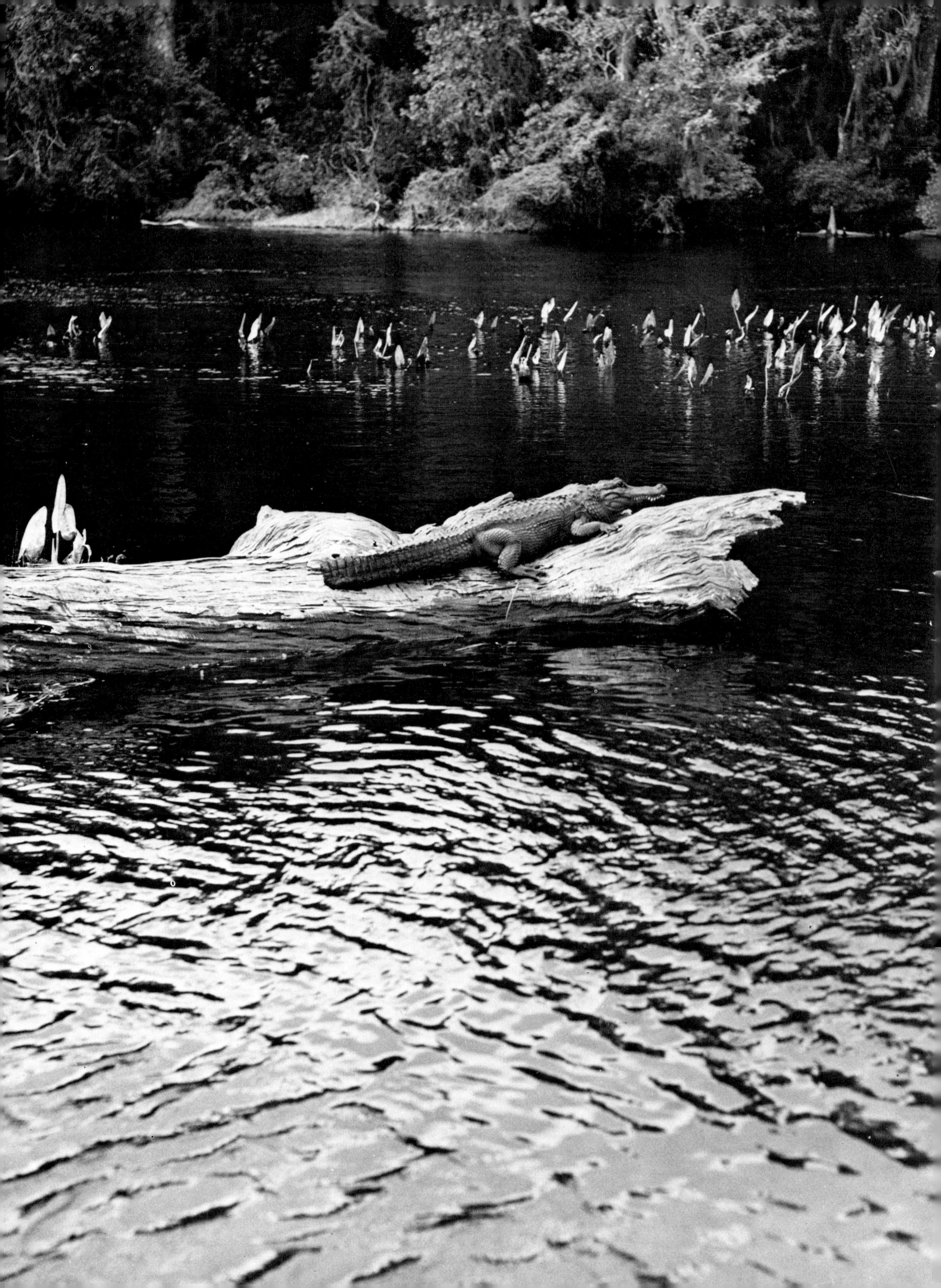

At Wakulla Springs, *left*, an alligator rests on a fallen tree trunk. A monument, *below*, marks the site of the Civil War battlefield of Natural Bridge, when Confederate militia and schoolboys repulsed a Union force attacking Tallahassee.

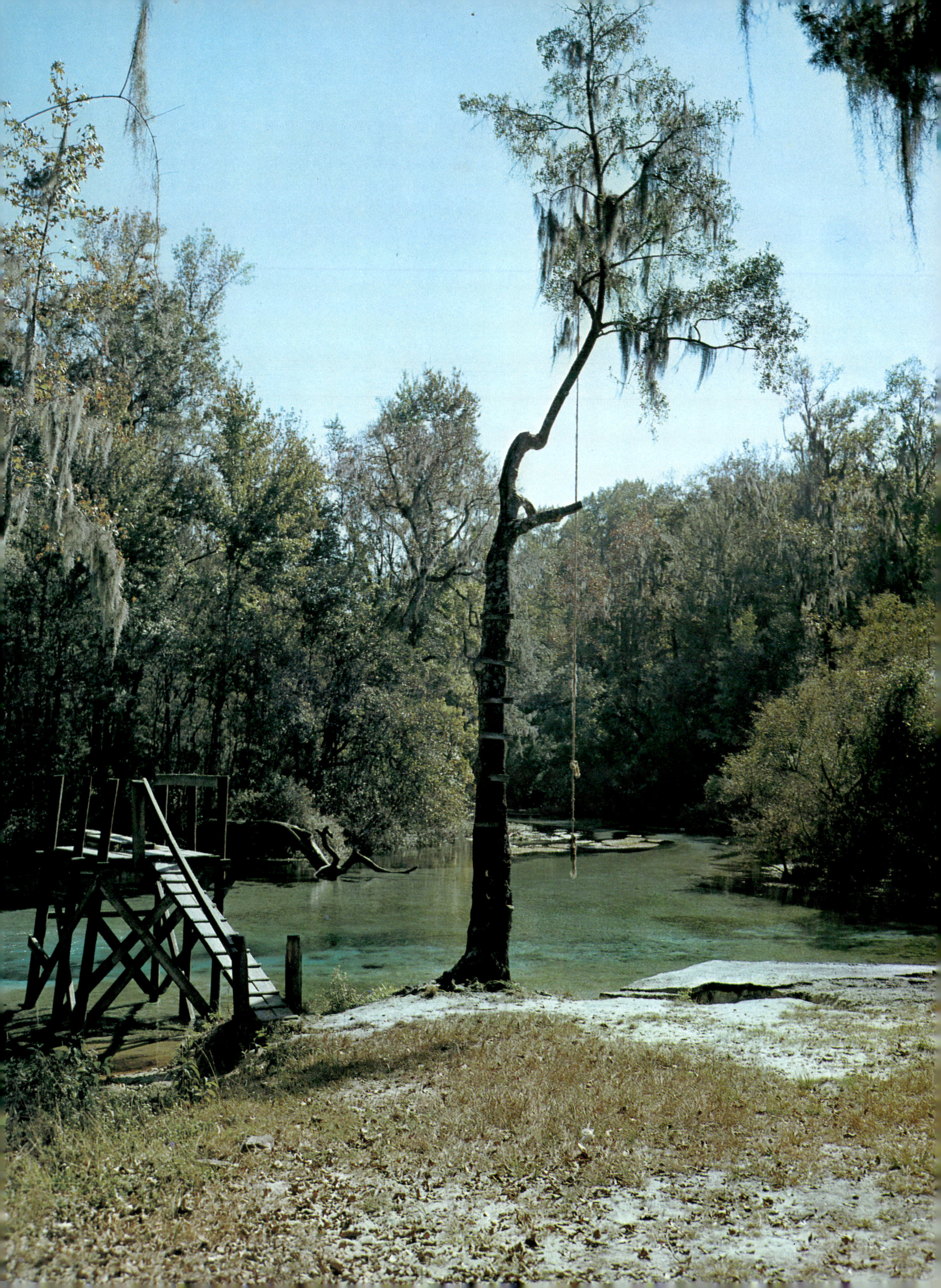

Left, a rural swimming hole—Blue Spring in Columbia County.
Below, an excursion boat takes tourists for a ride along the
Suwanee River at the Stephen Foster Memorial in White Springs.

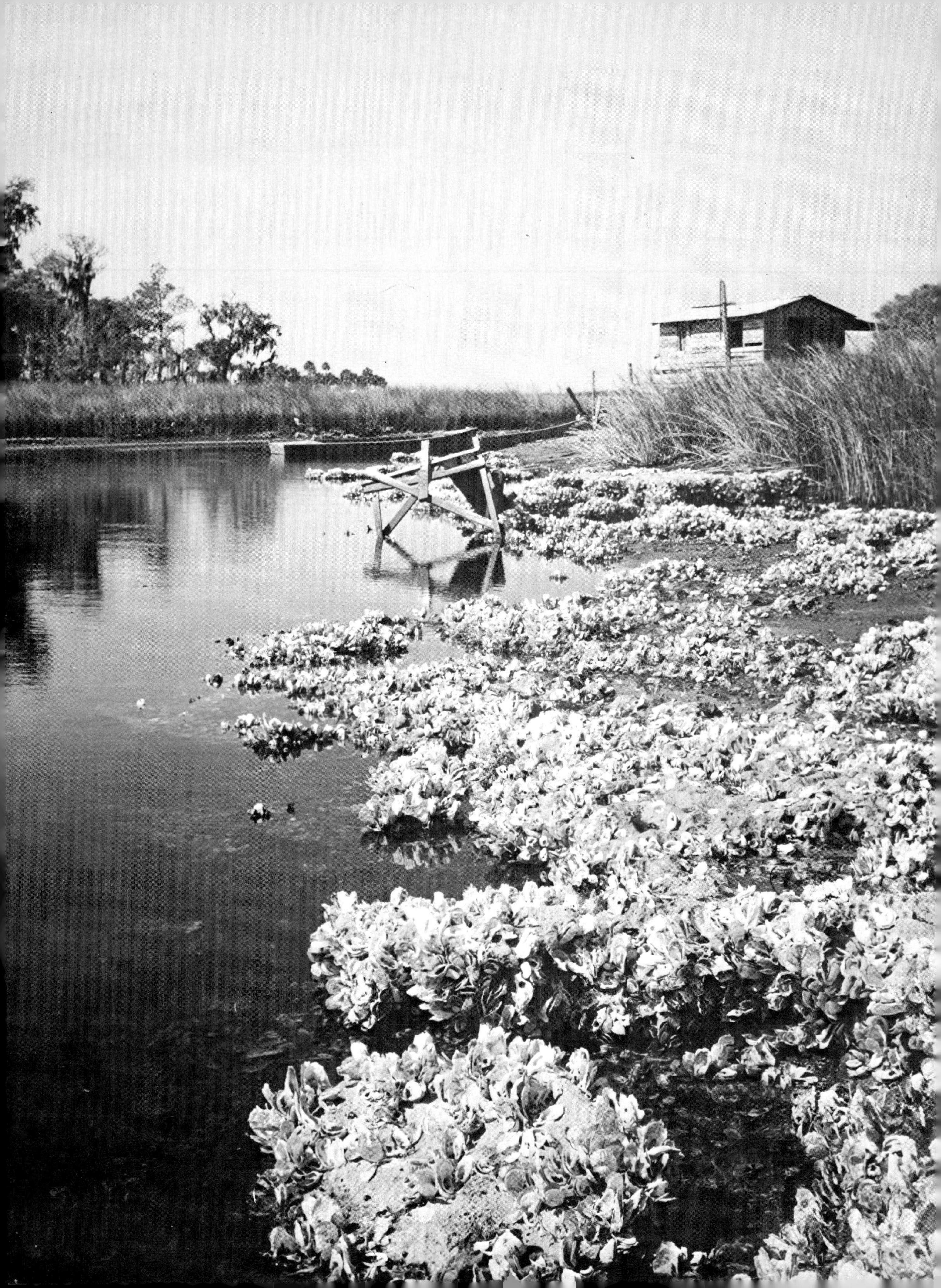

Olustee Battlefield monument, *upper left,* marks the site of a bloody Civil War battle. The Fernandina lighthouse, *upper right,* and Fort Clinch at Fernandina Beach (*above*) stand at the northernmost tip of Florida's Atlantic Coast. *Opposite,* Oyster clusters at low tide at the mouth of Spring Warrior Creek in Taylor County on the Gulf Coast.

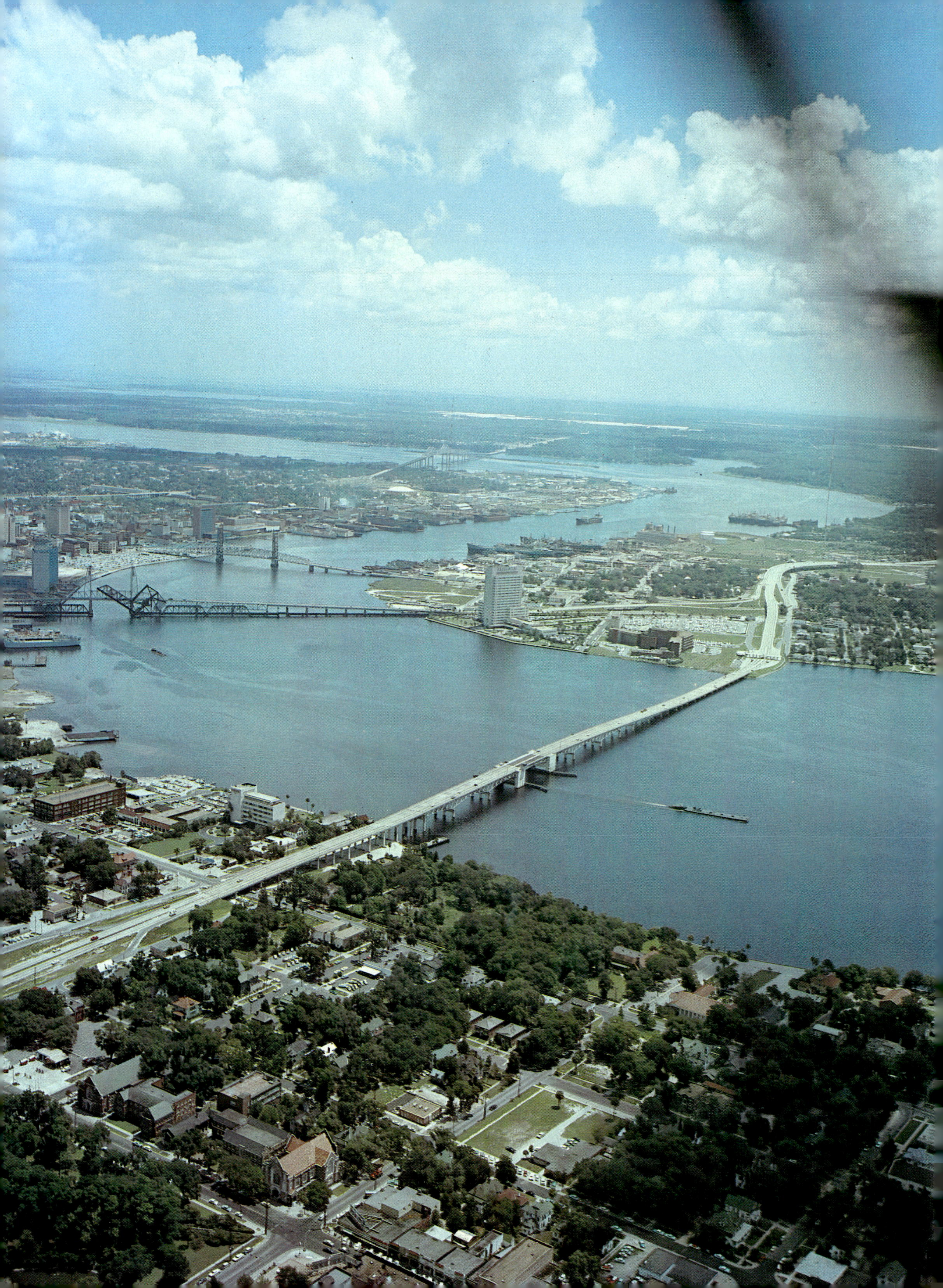

Opposite, the St. John's River winds past Jacksonville, Florida's most sprawling city. *At right*, the Jacksonville open air market; *below*, an illuminated riverside fountain with the city's skyline in the background.

Historic Kingsley plantation, *above*, stands on Fort George Island near Jacksonville. *Opposite*, the plantation's ruined slave quarters.

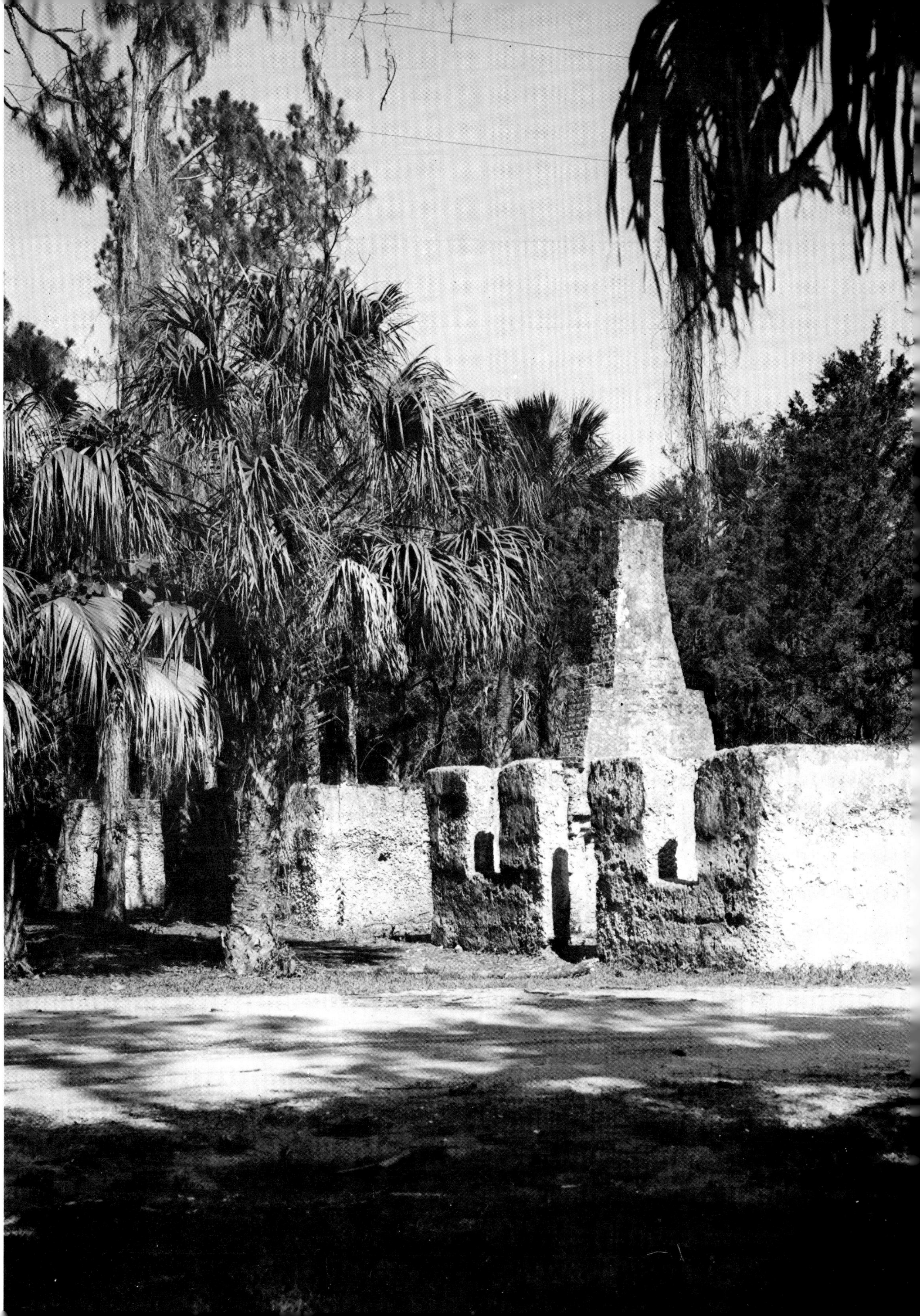

The nation's oldest city, St. Augustine, boasts the nation's oldest schoolhouse, *above*. Other attractions in the city include the oldest house *opposite*, and an old mill wheel, *left*.

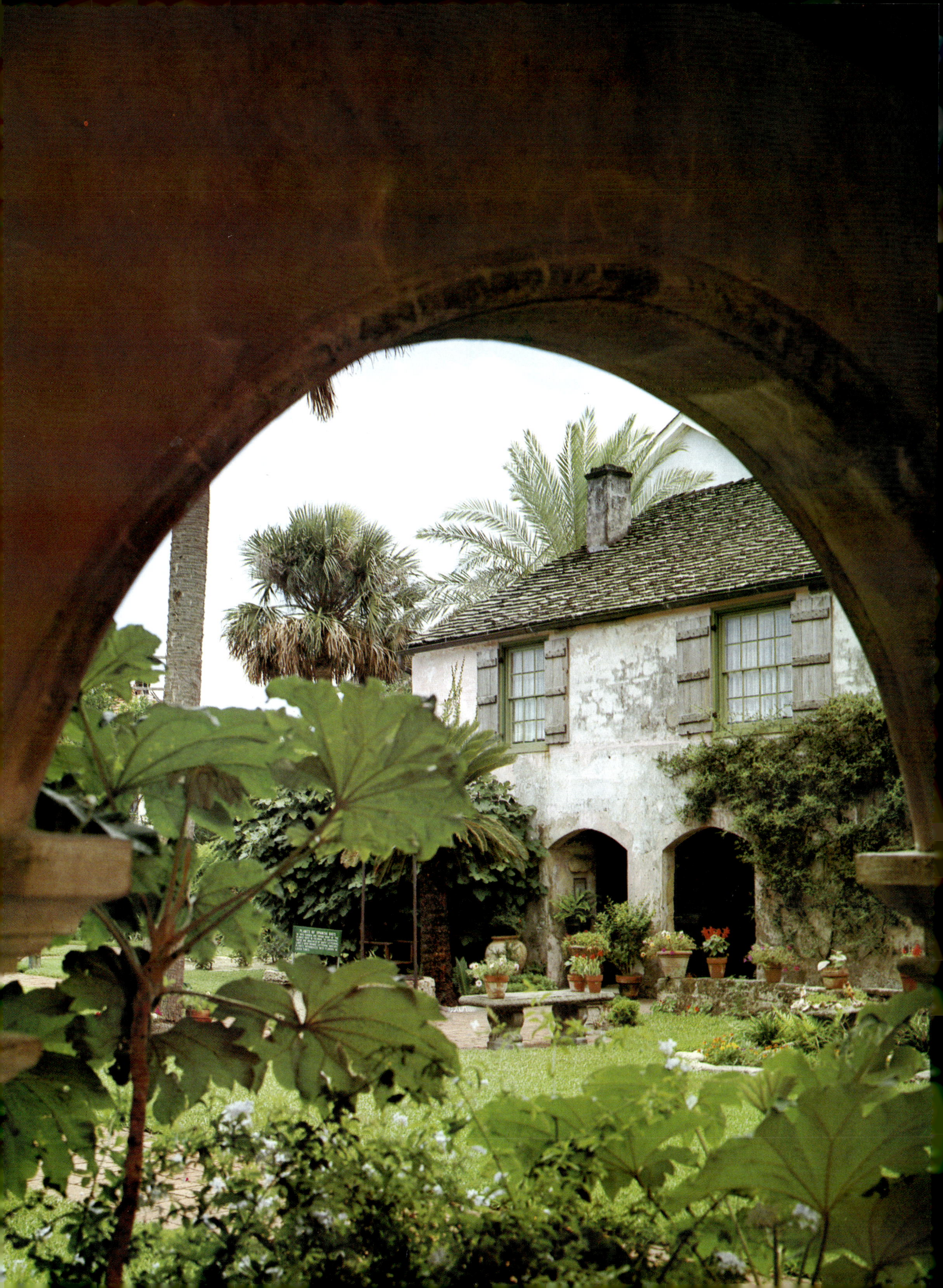

Construction of Castillo de San Marcos in St. Augustine, *above,* the oldest masonry fort in the United States, began in 1672. With walls nine feet thick at the top, the fort is surrounded by a moat and is approachable only by a drawbridge. *Opposite,* picturesque St. George Street in St. Augustine.

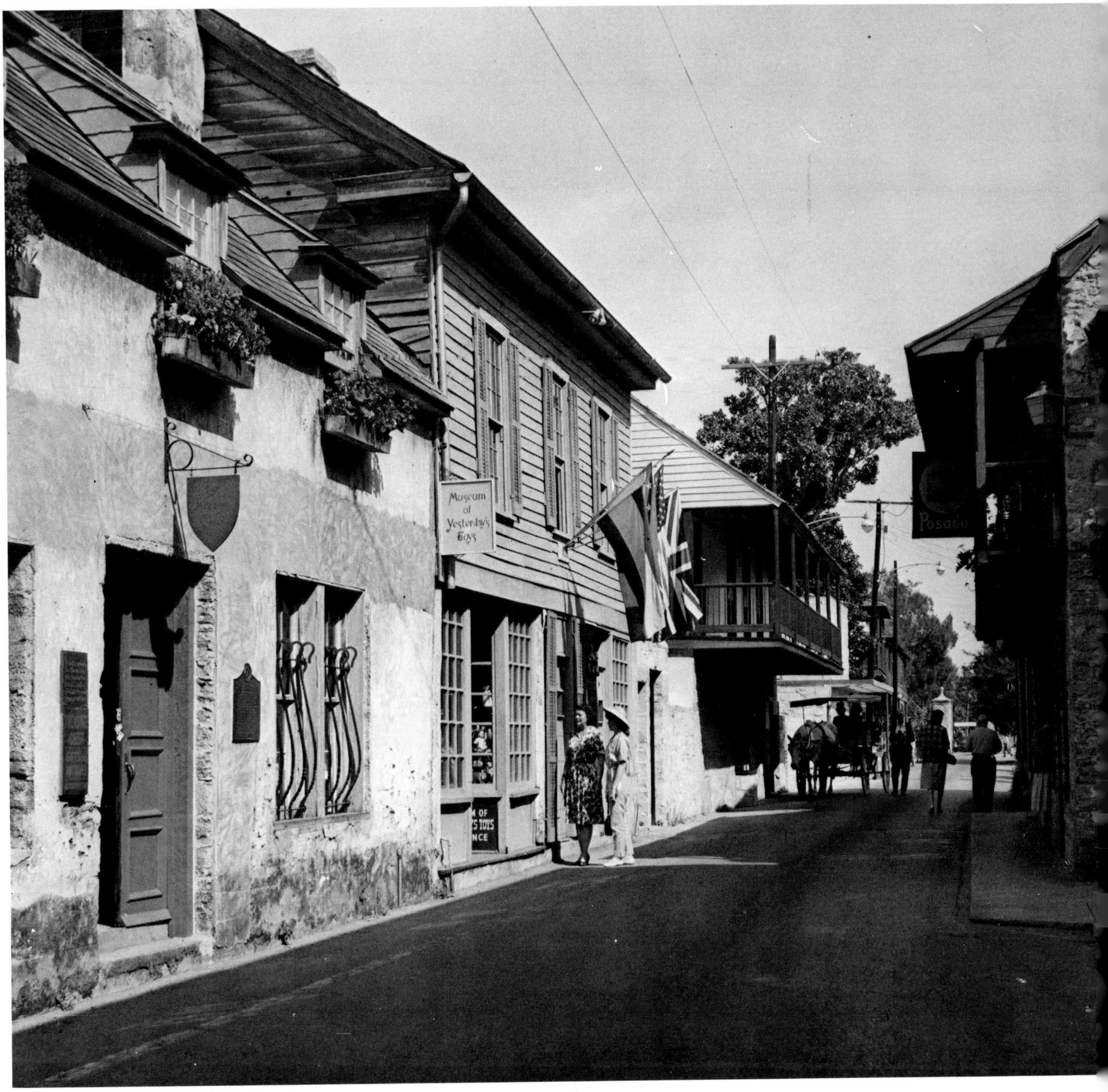
Museum of Yesterday's Toys
Posada

Above, the bright lights of an amusement park at Daytona Beach. *Opposite*, a vast housing development stretching across a barrier island at Ormond Beach.

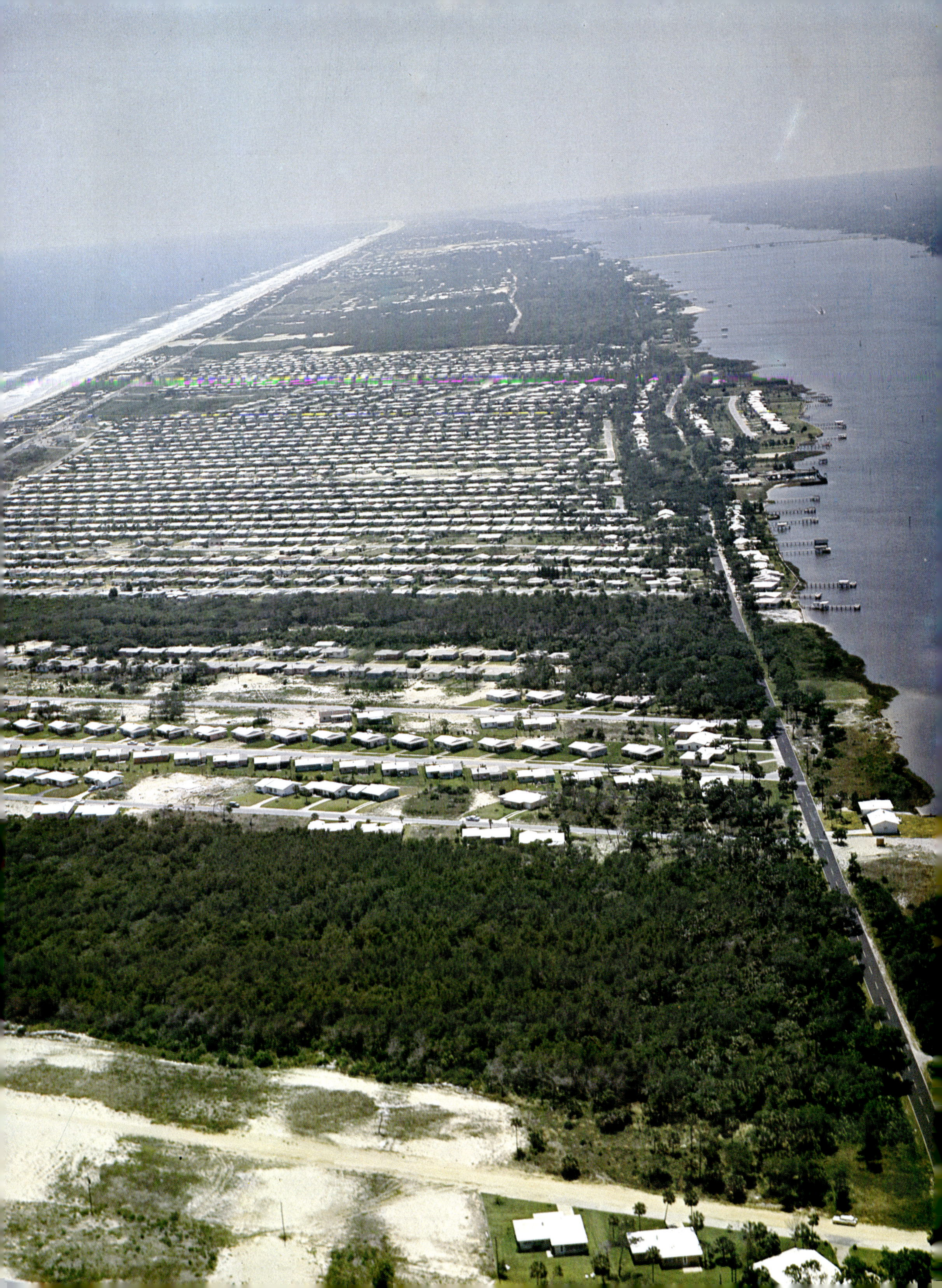

WORLD FAMOUS
ANAVERAL PIER
SURFING CAPITAL
RON JON
Surfboard
Showcase

Canaveral Pier, *below* at Cocoa Beach, reaches out into the Atlantic, within sight of the J. F. Kennedy Space Center. *At left*, Canaveral Light. *Opposite*, the ruins of an old sugar mill at New Smyrna Beach, destroyed during the Seminole Wars of the 1830's.

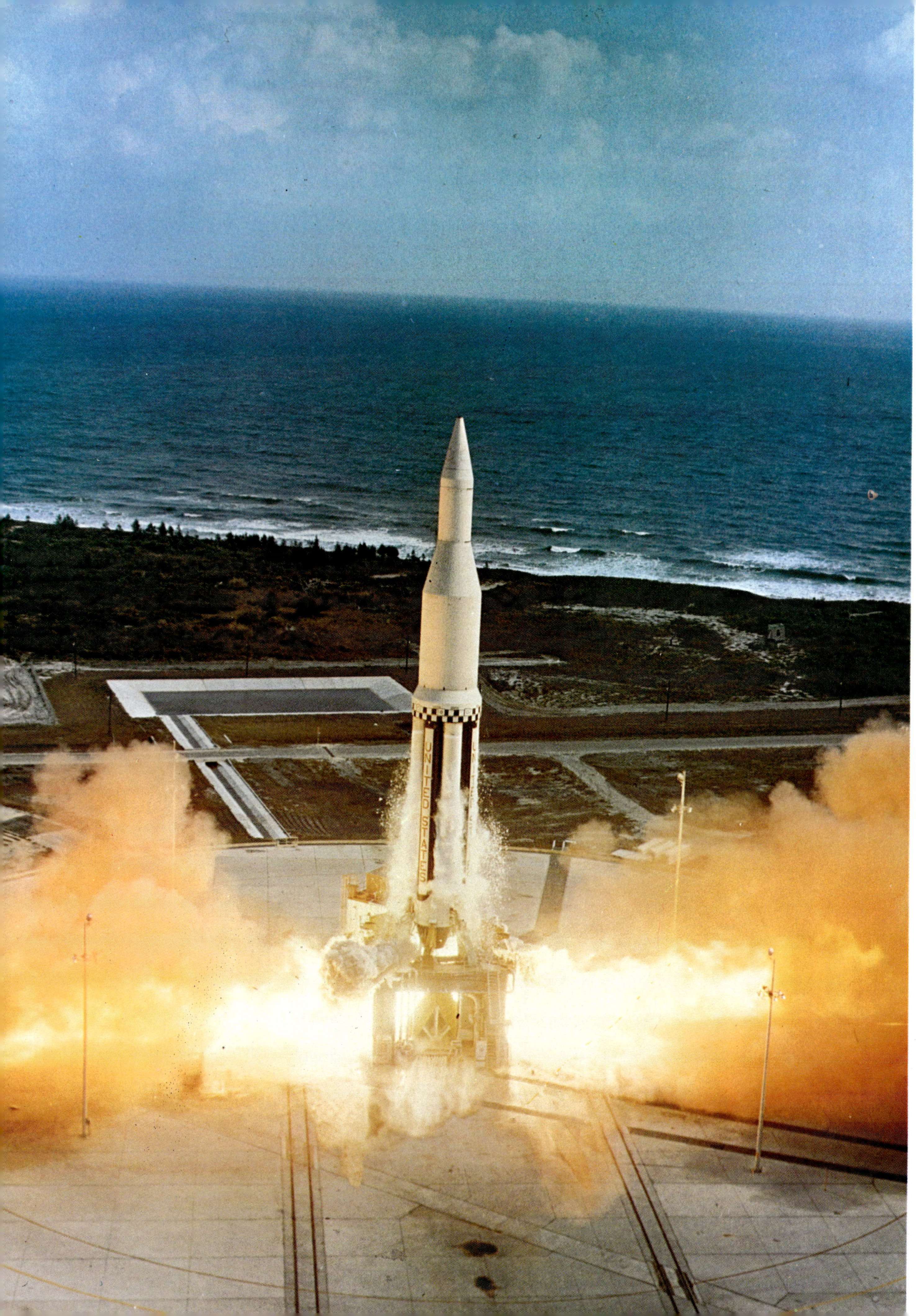
UNITED STATES

Cape Kennedy is the center of the United States space efforts. *Opposite,* the first Saturn space vehicle is launched. *Above,* the Vertical Assembly Building, reportedly the world's biggest building.

Three Florida houses: *At top*, the palm-fronted De Bary mansion near Sanford; *below*, the cottage at Cross Creek where the writer Marjorie Kinnan Rawlings wrote her books about Florida life. *Opposite*, a timeworn house in the small west coast town of Aripeka a few miles north of St. Petersburg.

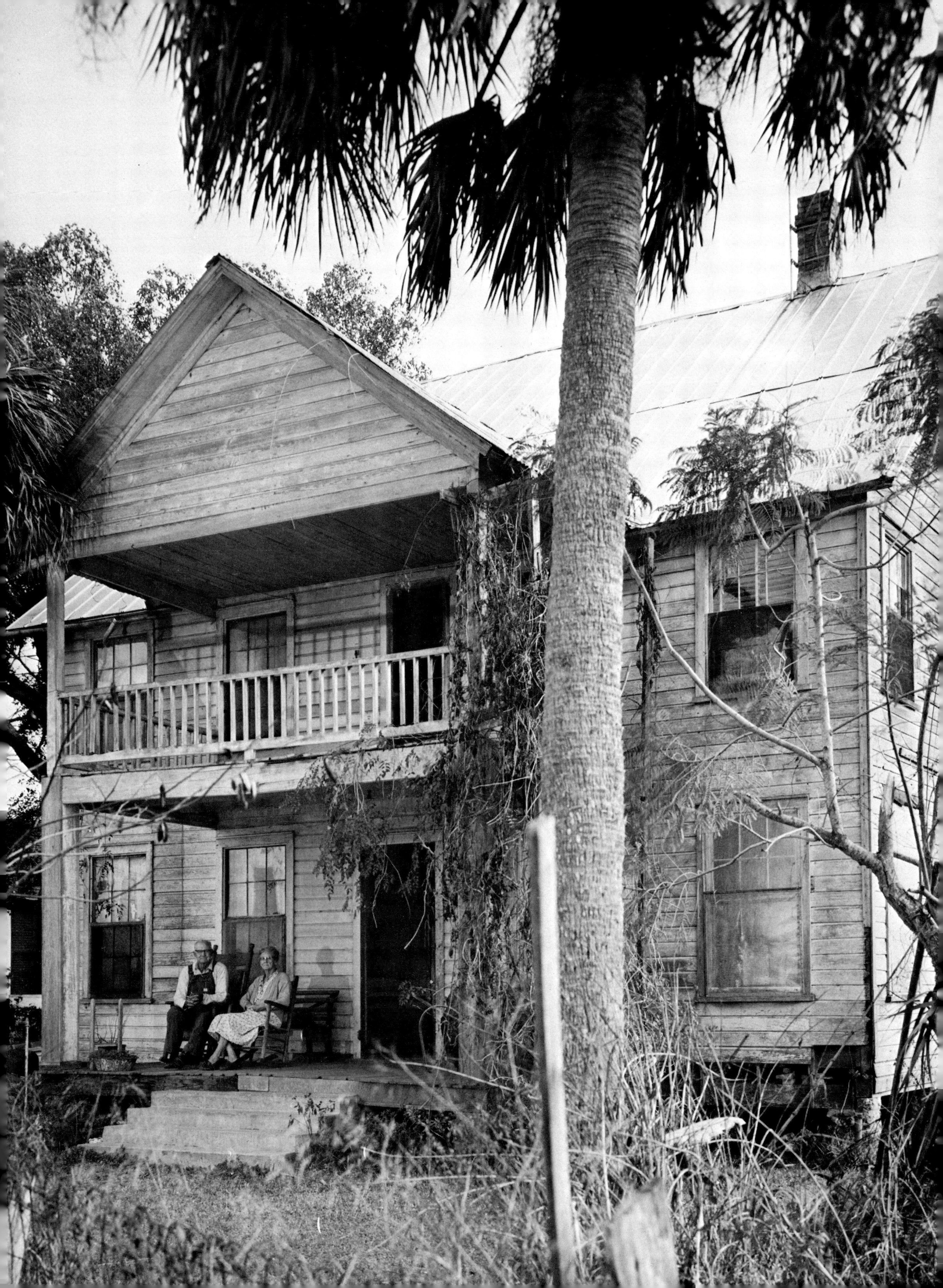

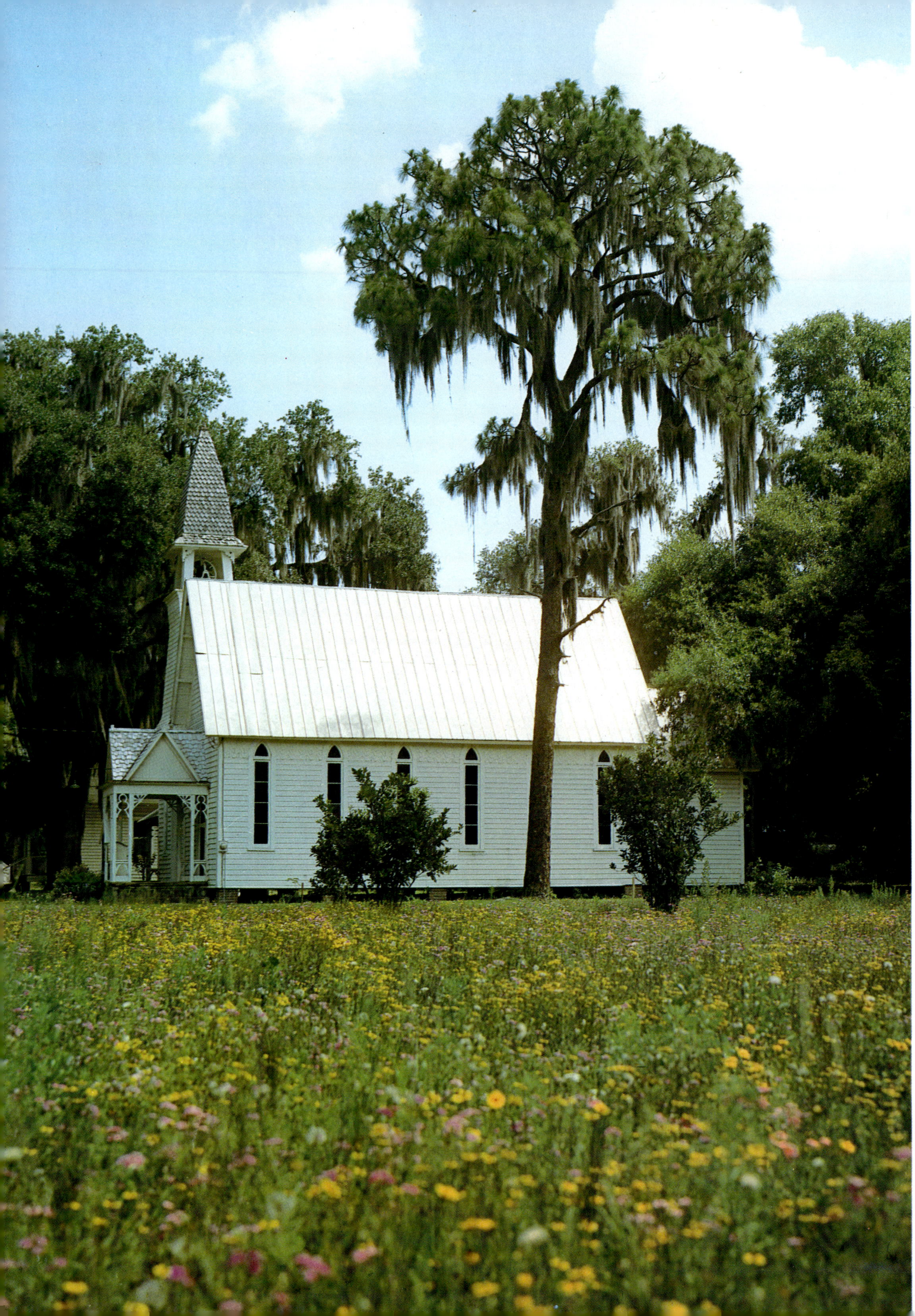

Opposite, in the small inland town of Welaka, a church stands next to a field of wildflowers. A few miles west of Welaka is Gainesville, home of the University of Florida. A wide-angle photograph, *above,* shows the university campus, with Century Tower and the auditorium in the foreground.

The central Florida city of Orlando, *below*, is dotted with small lakes. *At right*, the chapel of Rollins College in Winter Park.

Four views of Disney World: *At left (reading from the top)*, a copy of a German castle, a replica of Independence Hall; Saratoga style architecture on Main Street. *Below*, a sternwheeler.

Above, Iron Mountain Lake, in the lake region of Central Florida. *Opposite,* the famous Bok Singing Tower at Lake Wales.

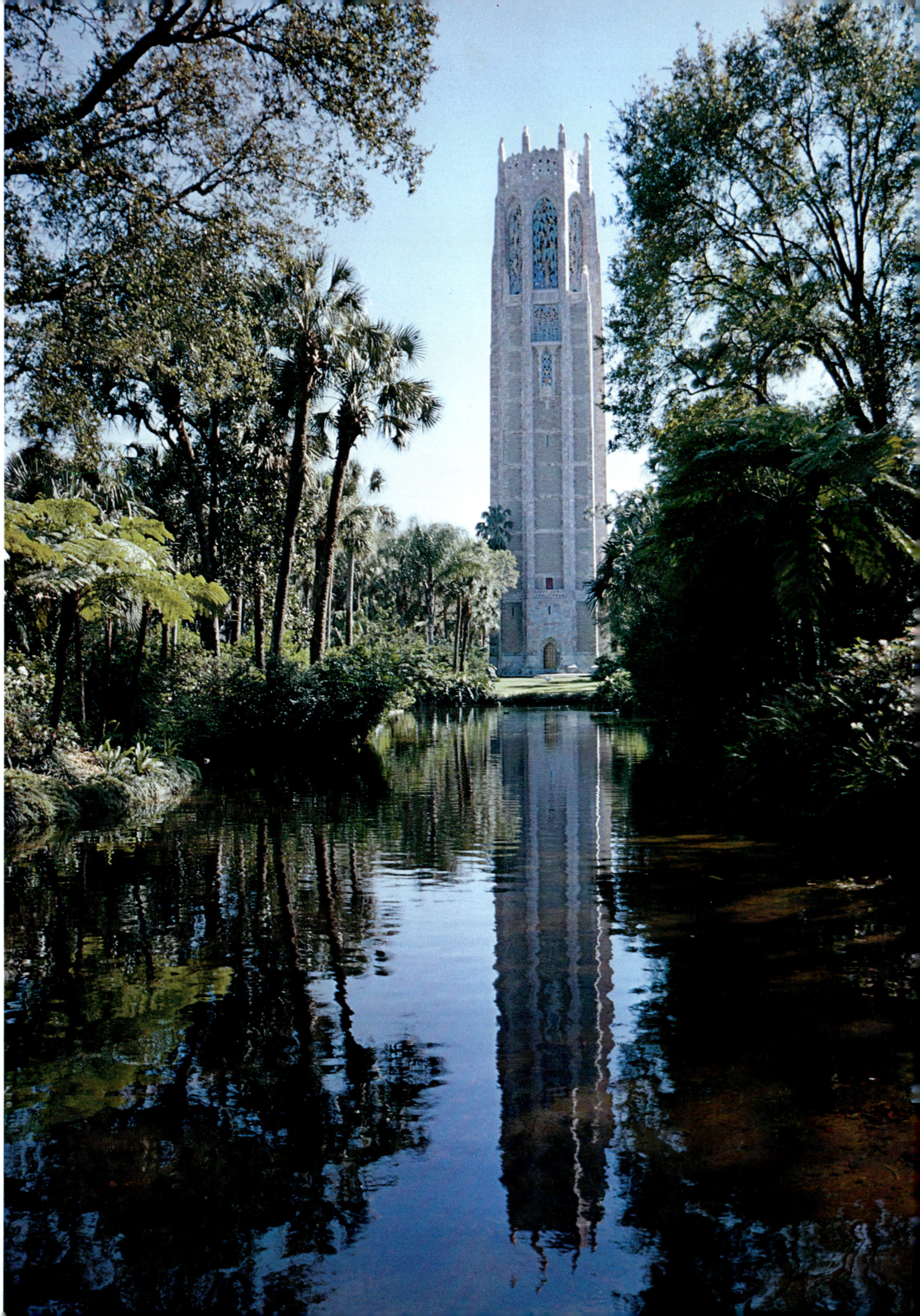

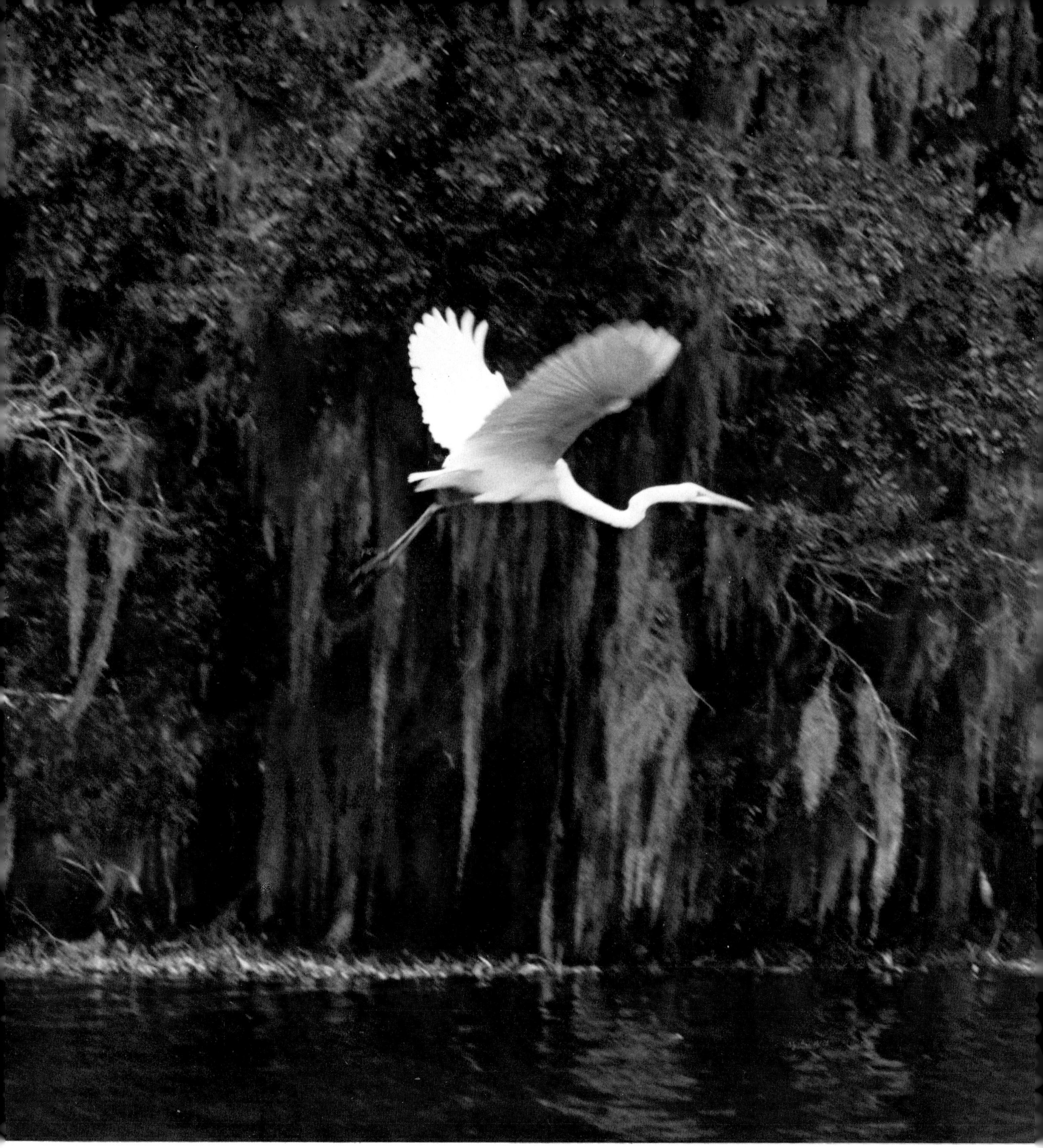

Opposite, at Orange Lake, north of Ocala, an egret flies over the rippling water. *Above*, lily pads on Manatee Springs in Levy County in the thinly populated Big Bend region.

Overleaf, groves of citrus trees stretch as far as the eye can see from the top of the Citrus Tower near Clermont in central Florida's citrus country.

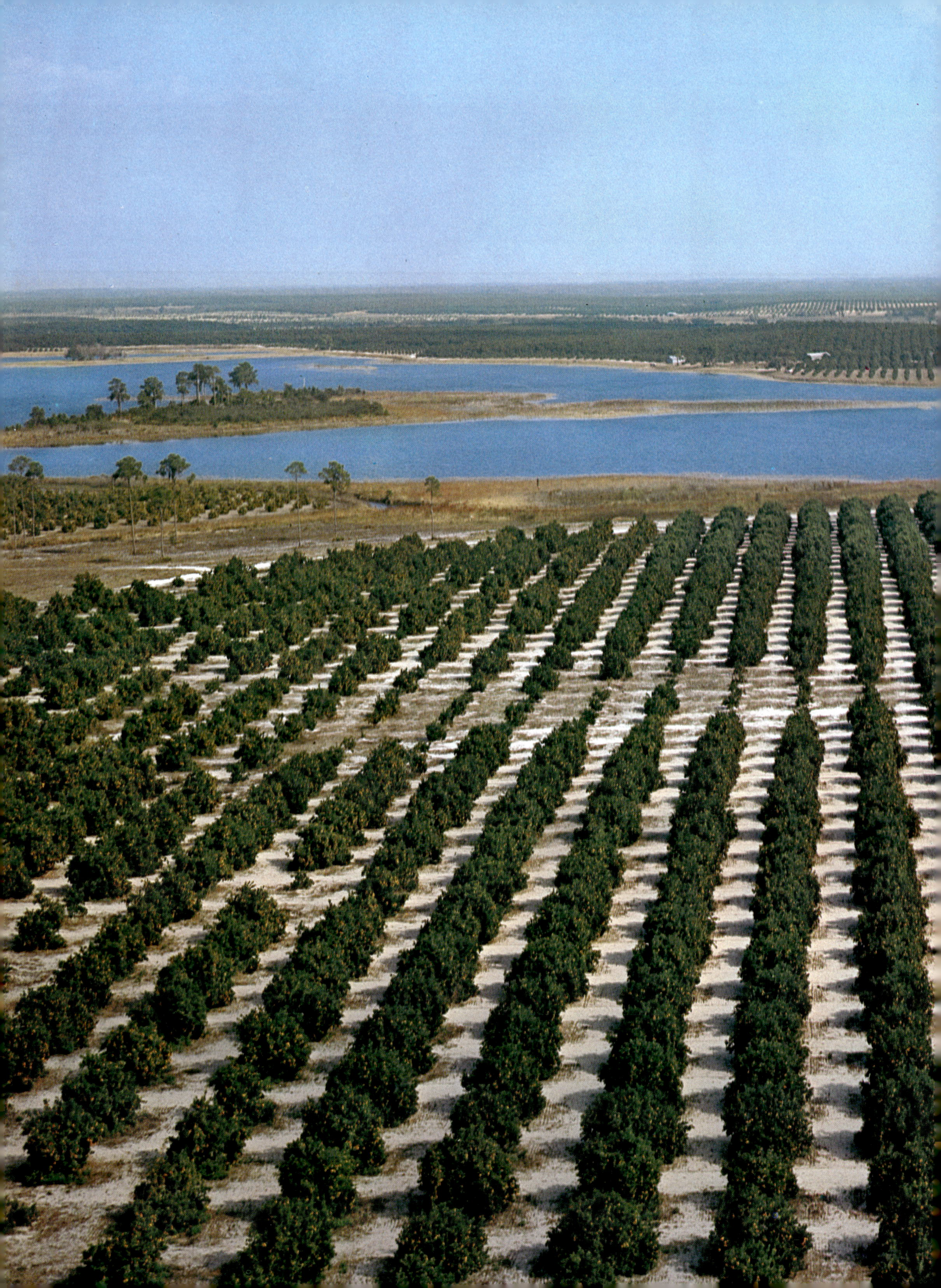

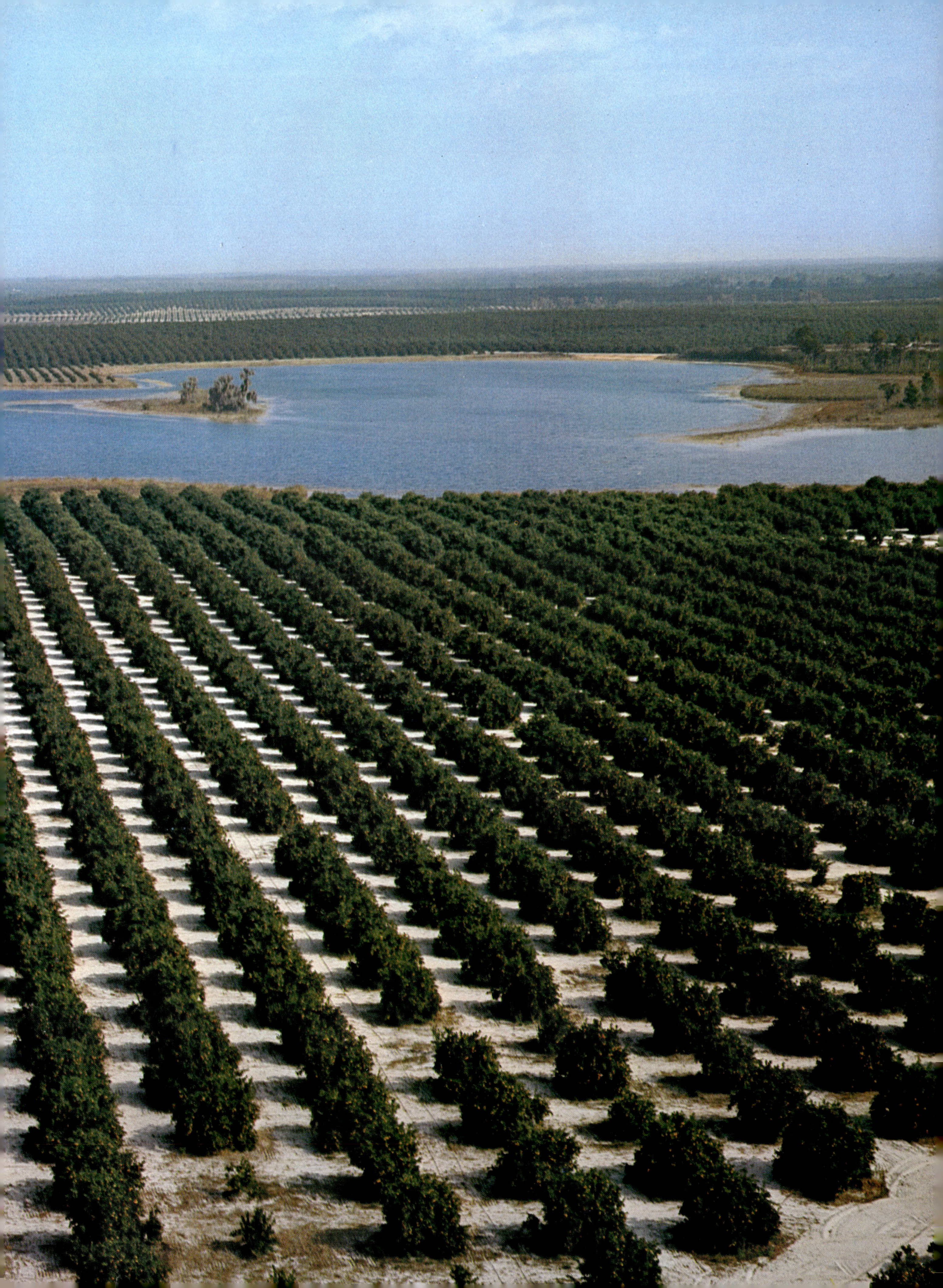

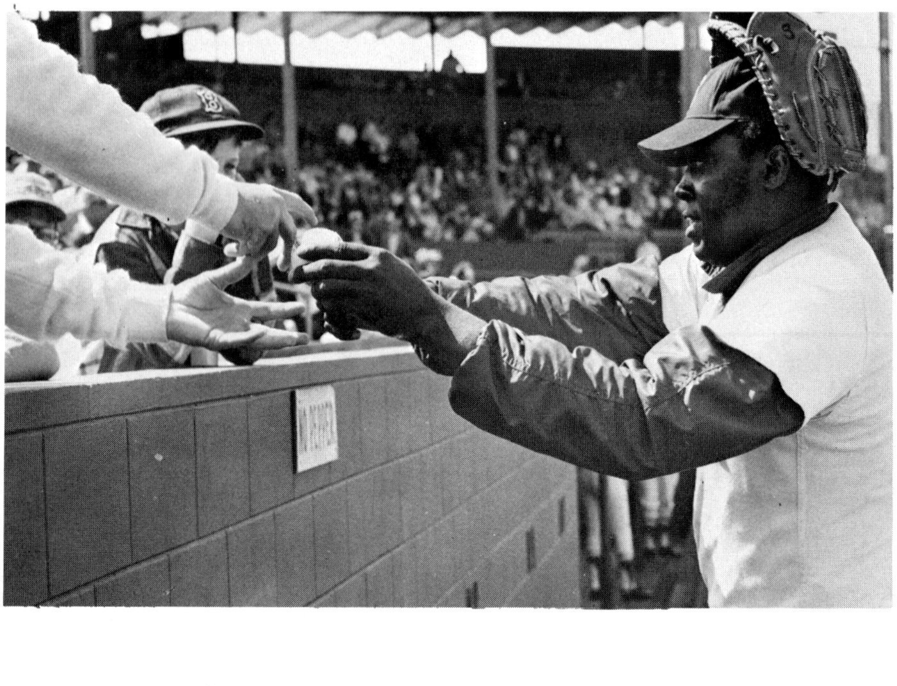

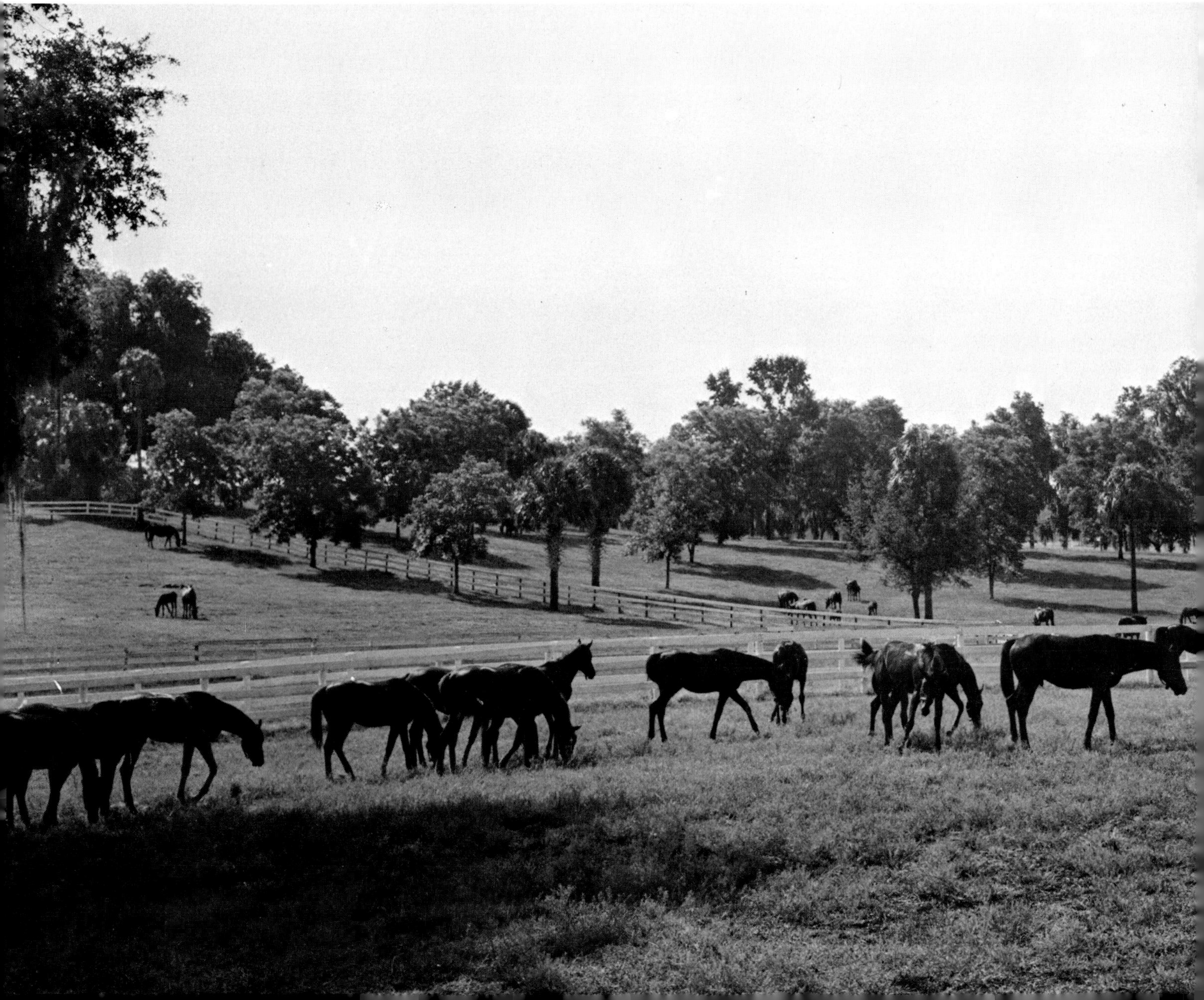

Horse farms, such as the one below, abound in the region around Ocala. *At left,* a Red Sox ballplayer autographs a baseball for a fan at the Red Sox headquarters at Winter Haven. The monument at Kissimmee, *right,* is made of stones from every state and twenty-one foreign lands.

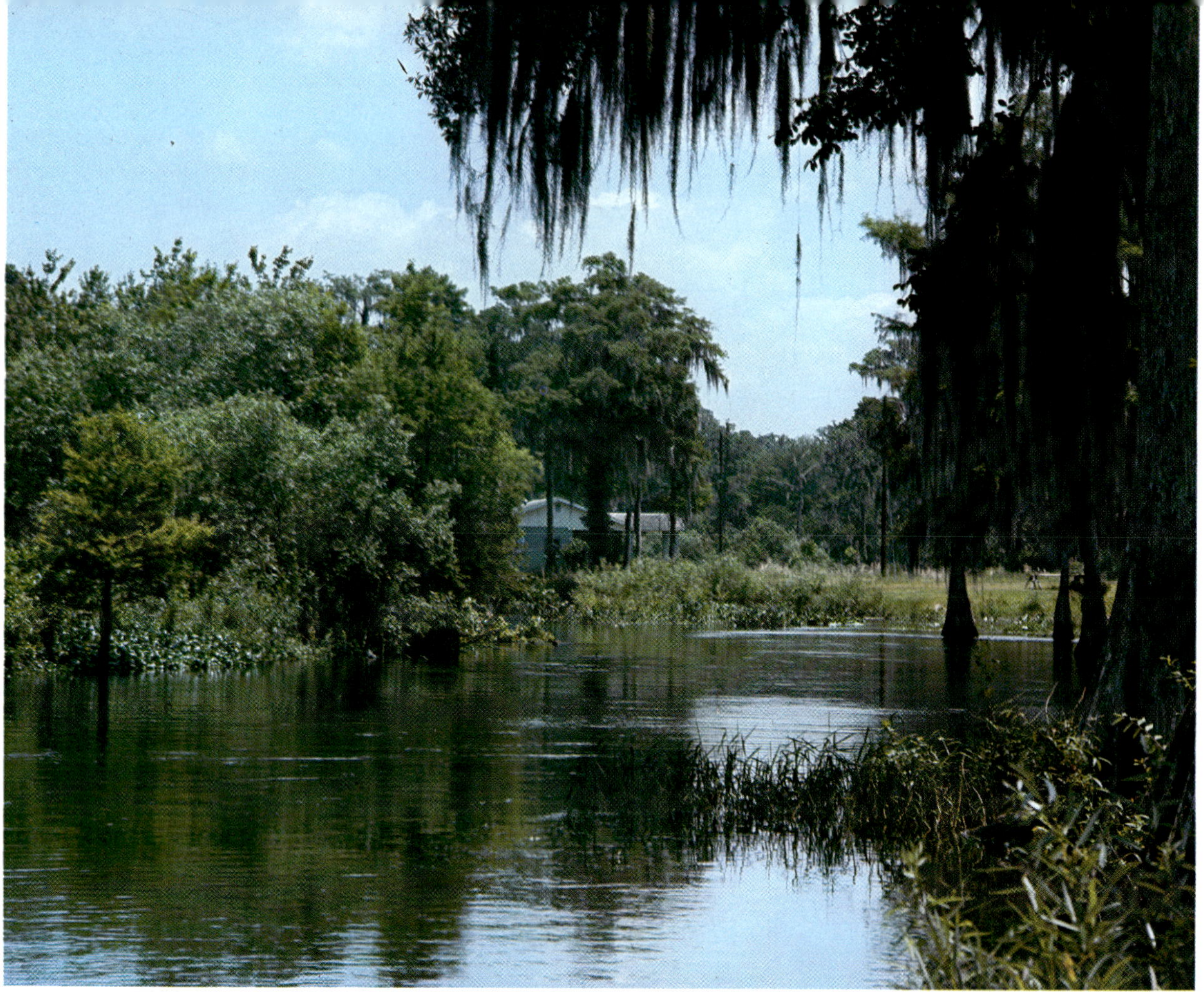

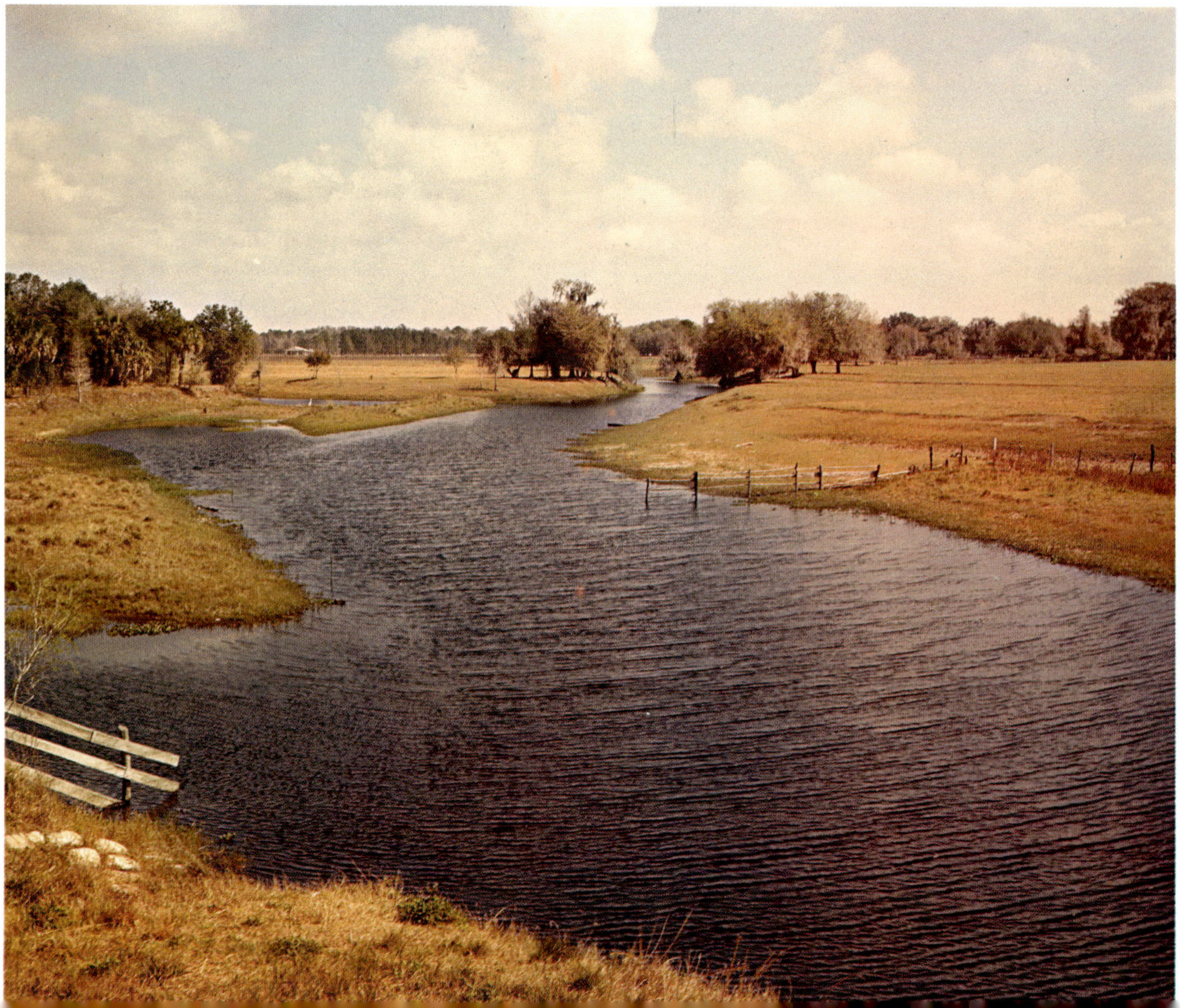

Above, Spanish moss on a live oak tree in Withlacoochee State Forest.
Opposite, two central Florida rivers: the Withlacoochee, *at top*, and the Kissimmee.

The quaint old island town of Cedar Key, *above*, on the Gulf of Mexico was once a bustling port. Cedar Key is famous for its seafood (*opposite*, two of the town's restaurants) and its old houses, such as the one on the opposite page.

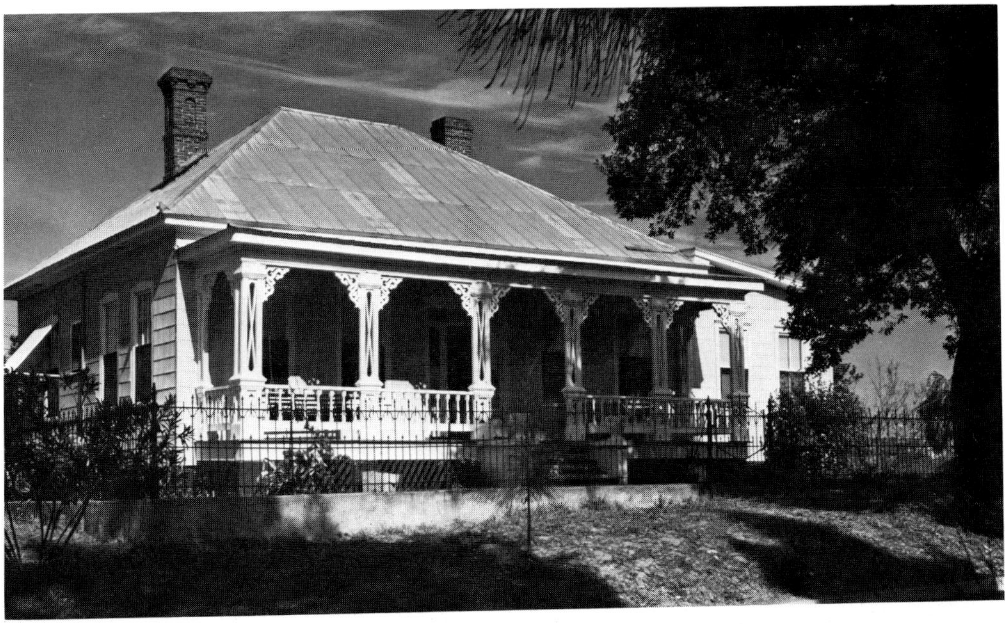

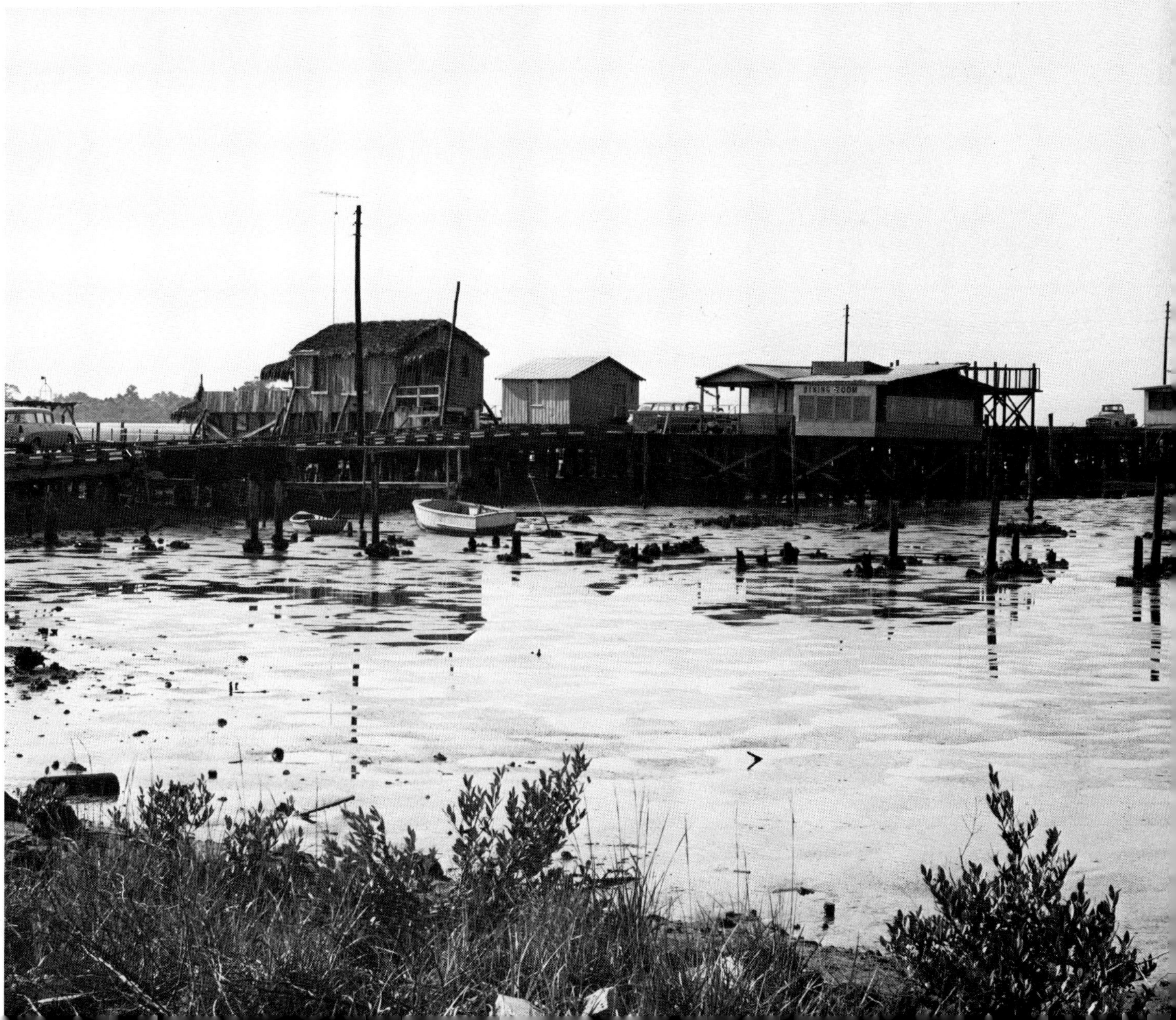

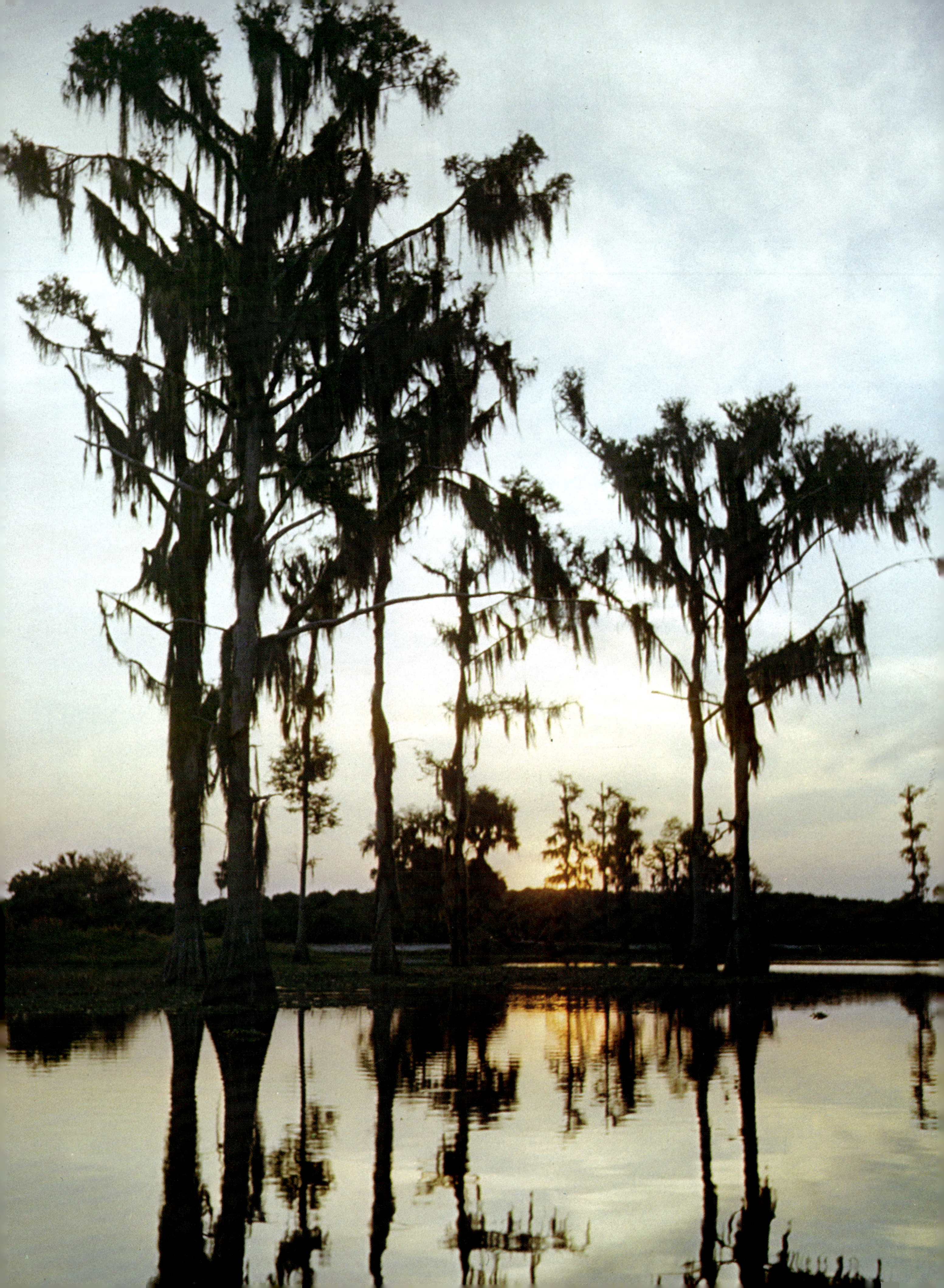

South of Tampa, at Ellenton, lies the Gamble mansion, *above,* Florida's only Confederate shrine, an old plantation house where the Confederate Secretary of State, Judah P. Benjamin, hid from federal troops. *Opposite,* Lake Tsala Popka.

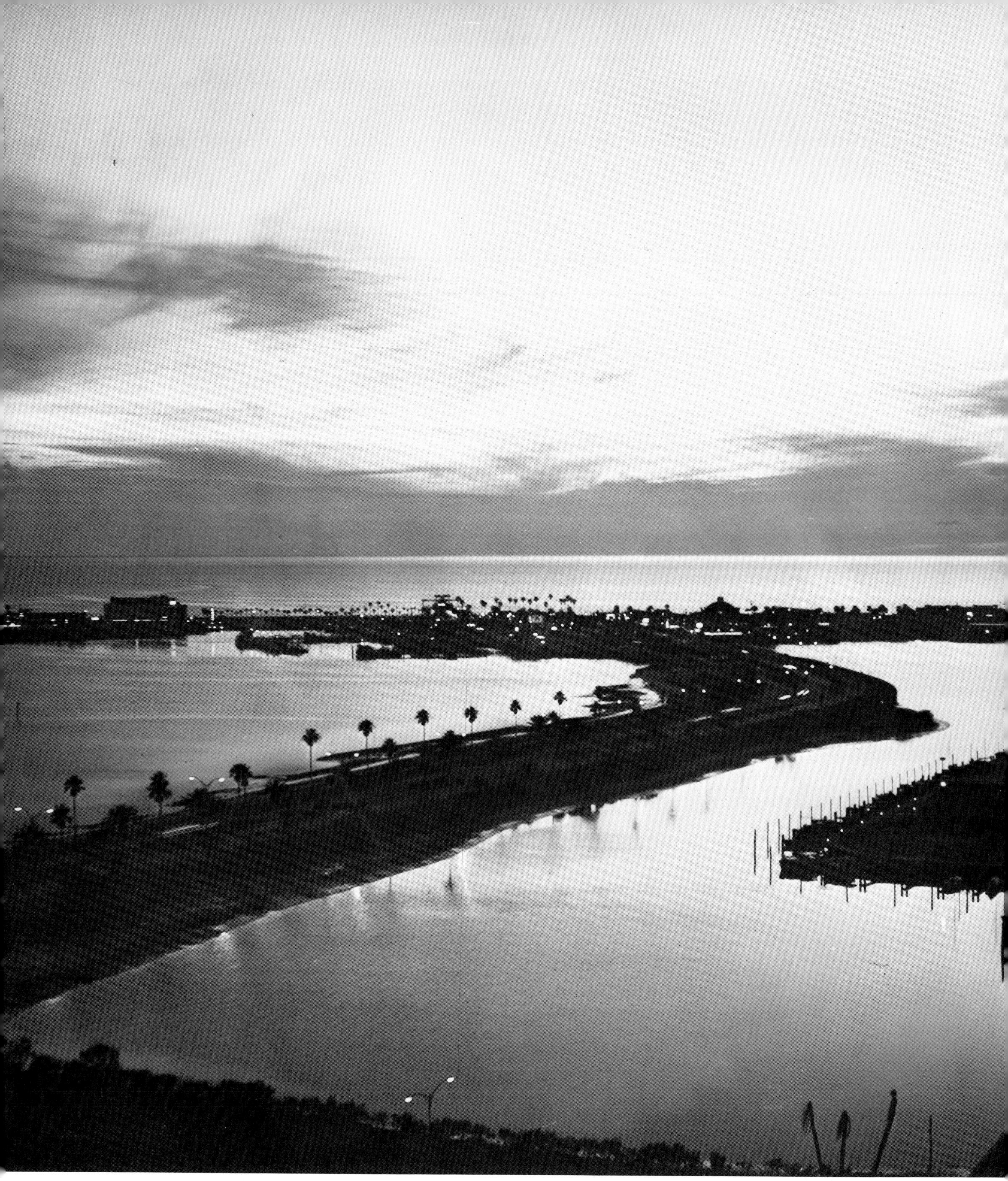

A palm-lined causeway, *left*, connects Clearwater with Clearwater Beach. A few miles north is the sponge-fishing town of Tarpon Springs, with a large population of Greek-Americans. *Below*, the town's icon-decorated and domed Greek Orthodox Church.

Dressed in Spanish costume,
a man and two women, *right*,
greet tourists in Tampa's
Ybor City, the old Latin quarter.
Below, a sunset at Clearwater.
Opposite, sponge fishers' boats
at Tarpon Springs.

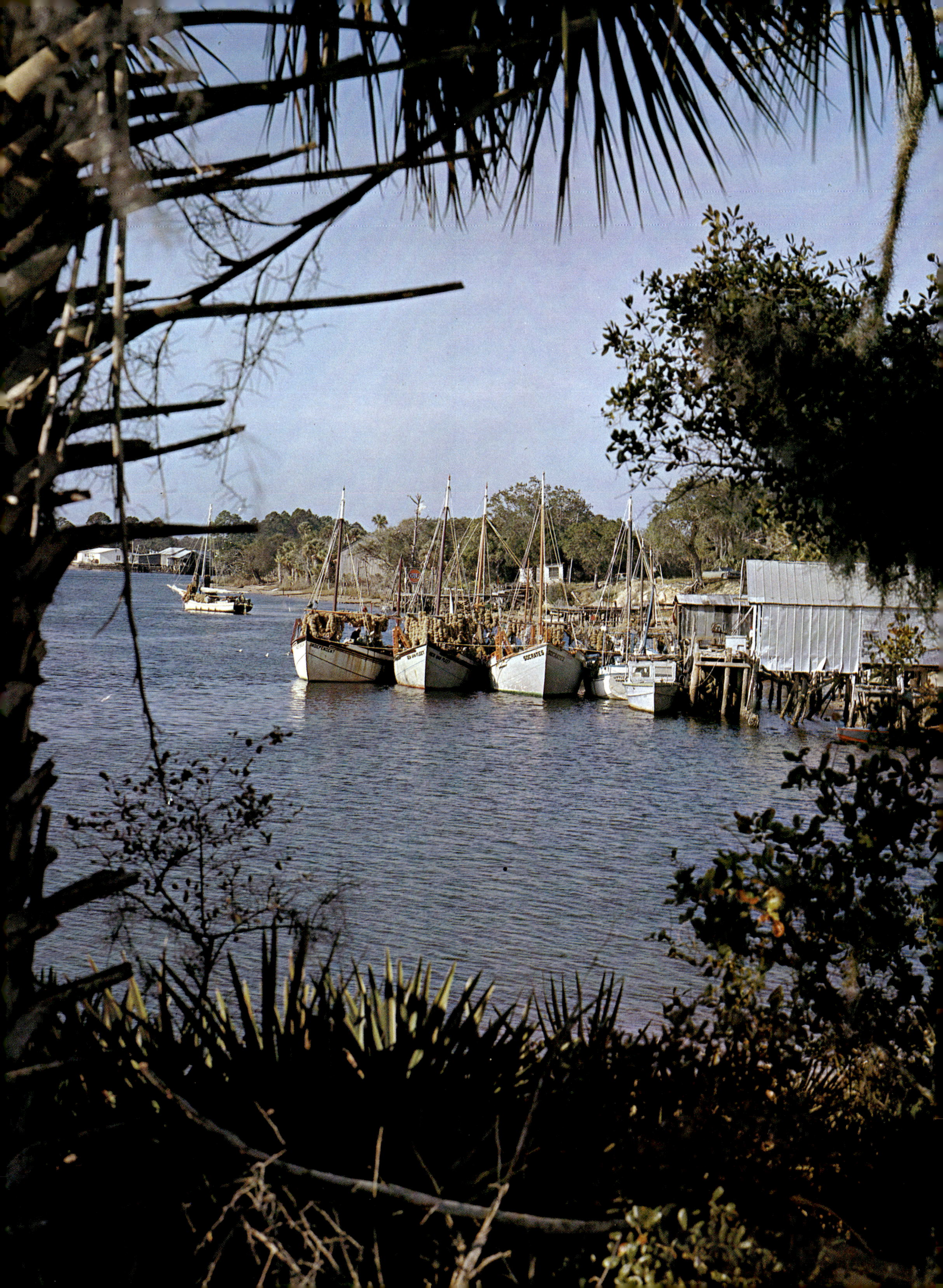

100

The University of Tampa's onion domes, *left*, line the Hillsborough River in downtown Tampa. The chapel at nearby Florida Southern College, *opposite*, was designed by Frank Lloyd Wright. *Below*, another unusual modern building: Sarasota's waterfront Hall of Performing Arts.

St. Petersburg Beach stretches across the foreground in this aerial view of the St. Petersburg region.

Pages 104–05, Rapids in Hillsborough River State Park, northeast of Tampa.

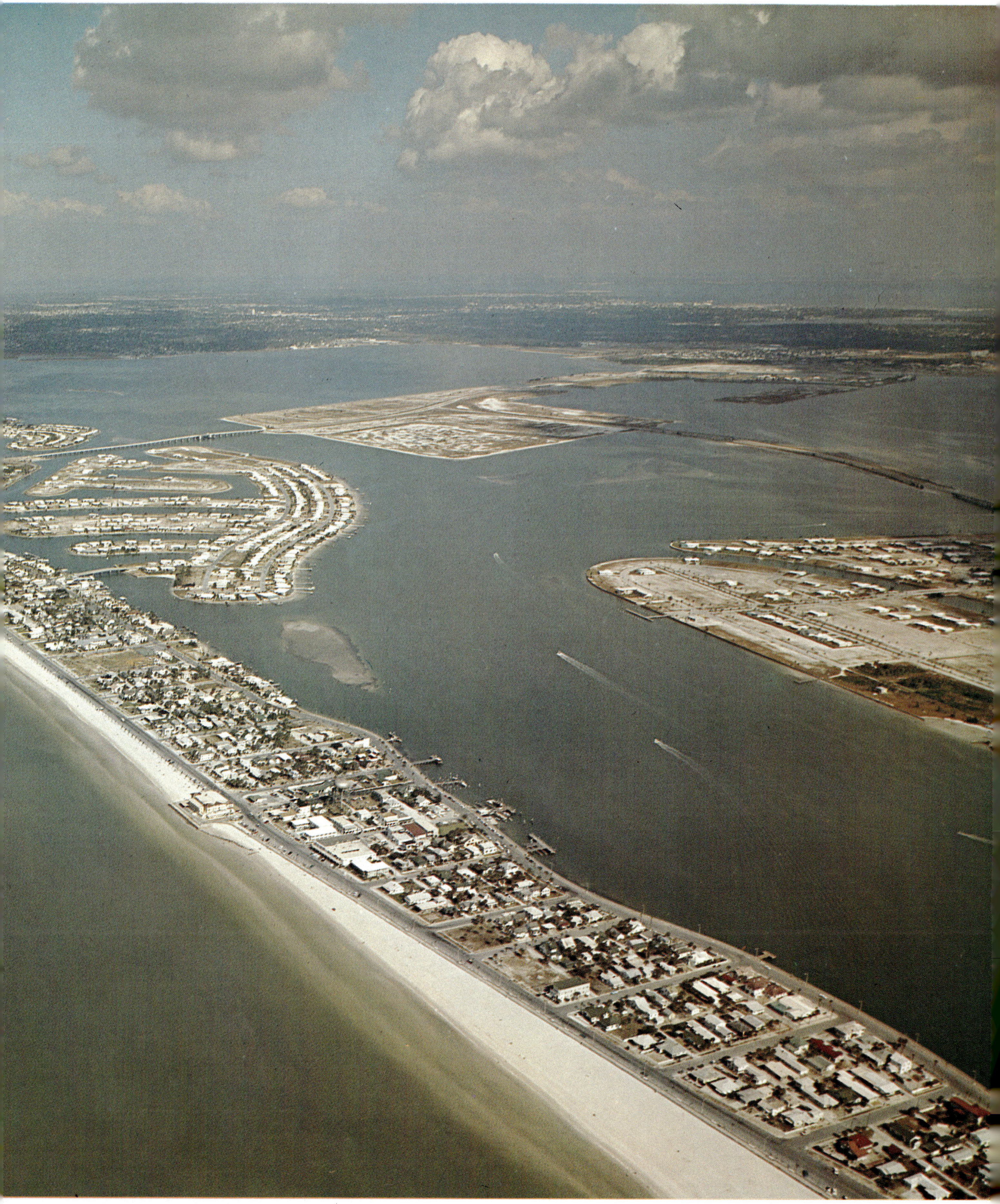

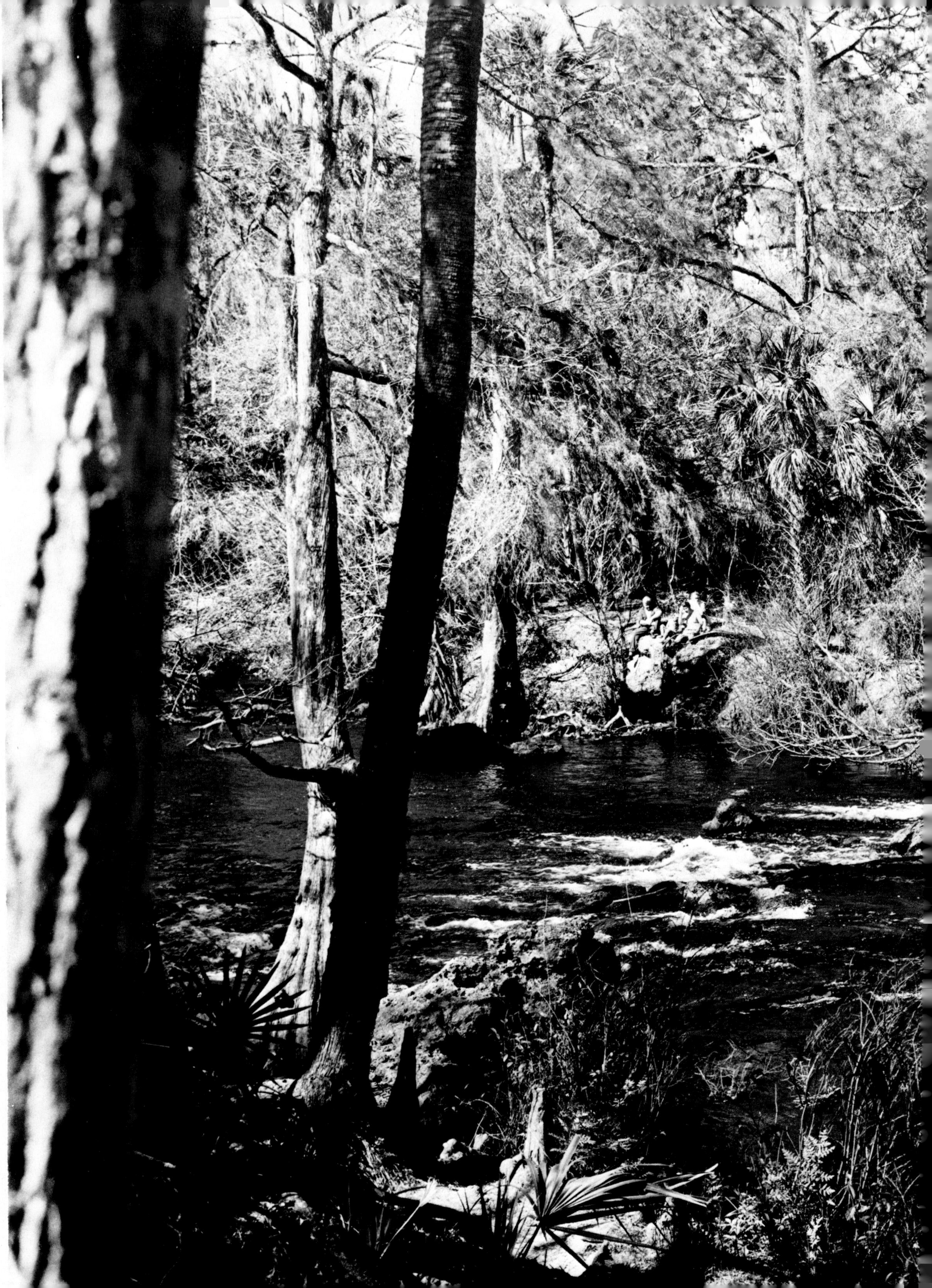

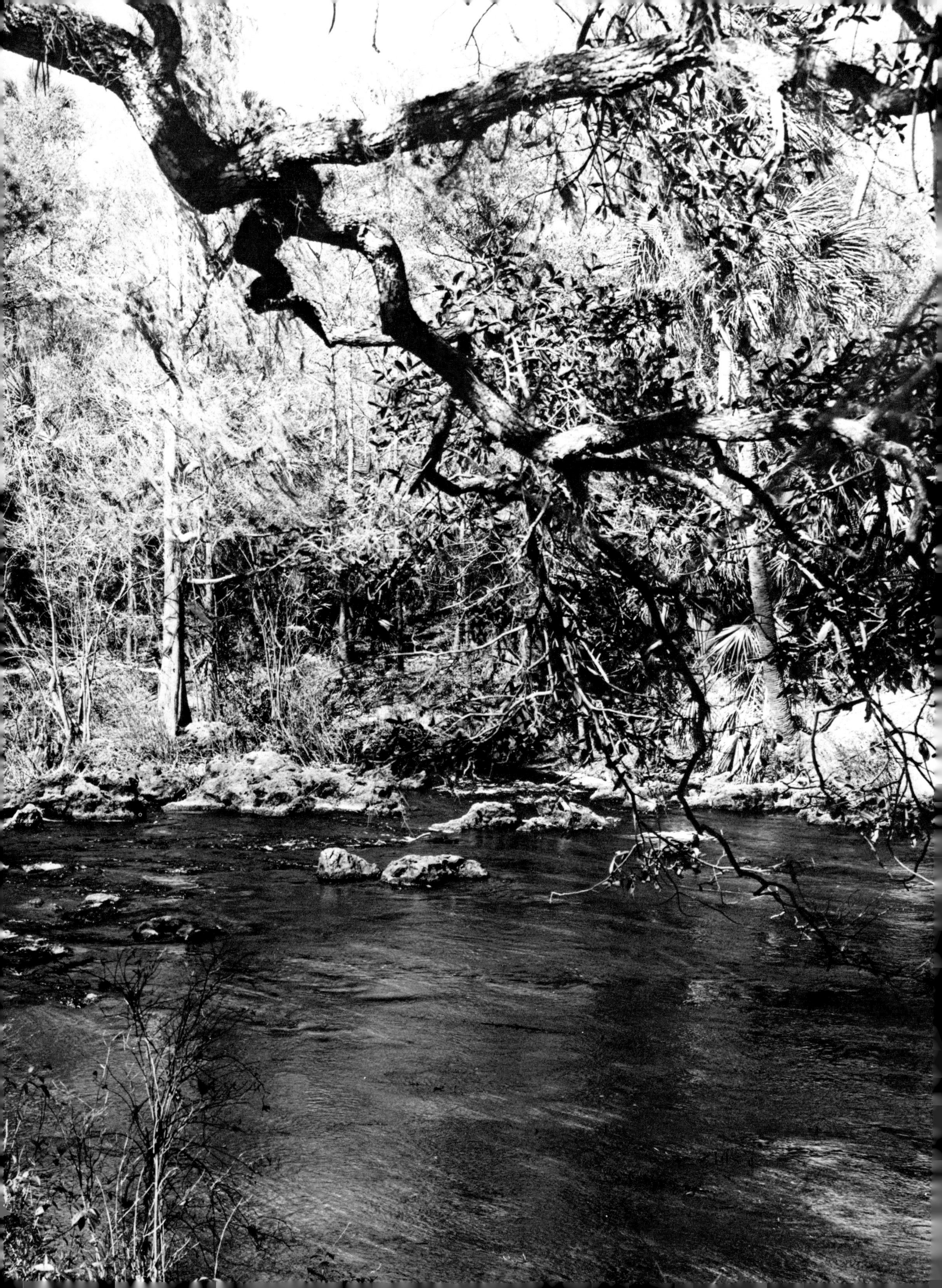

While their elders sail larger boats, youngsters in eight-foot "optimist prams"—
a boat that originated in Florida—participate in a regatta at Sarasota.

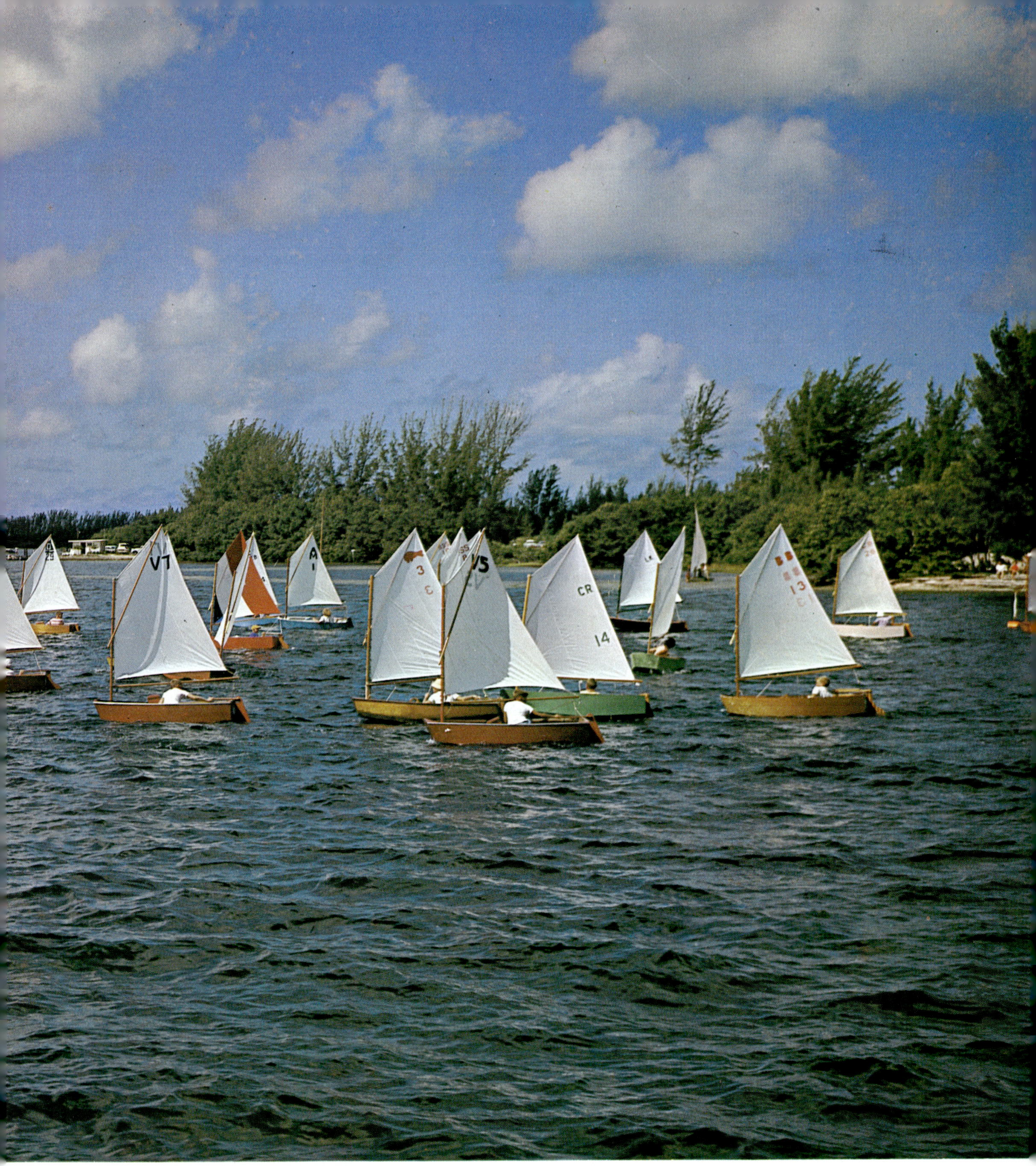
V7
V5
CR
14

The Ringling Museum in Sarasota, *above*, is built in an Italian Renaissance style. *Opposite*, the sculpture-studded garden of the museum. *At right*, a statue of a dwarf.

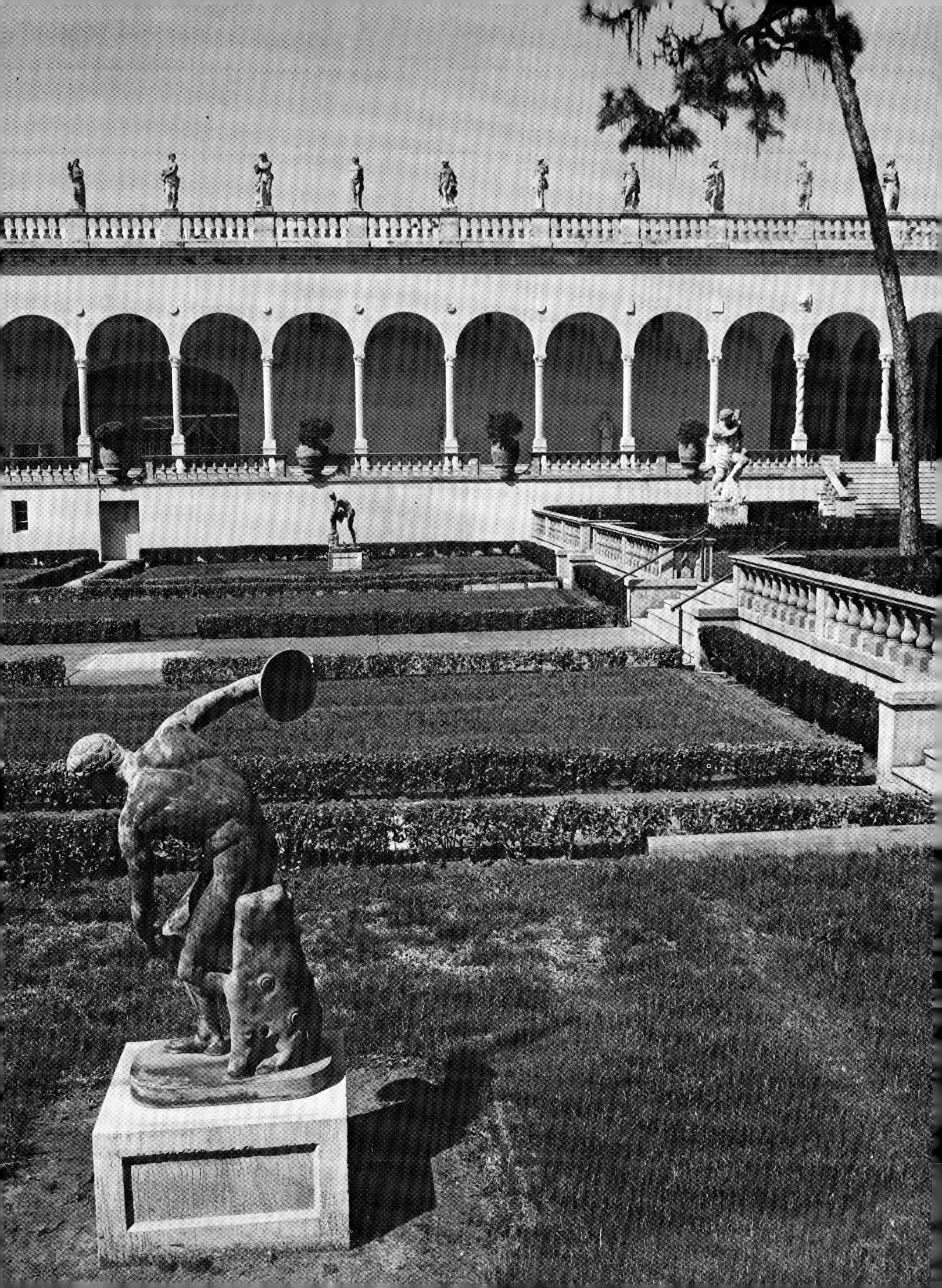

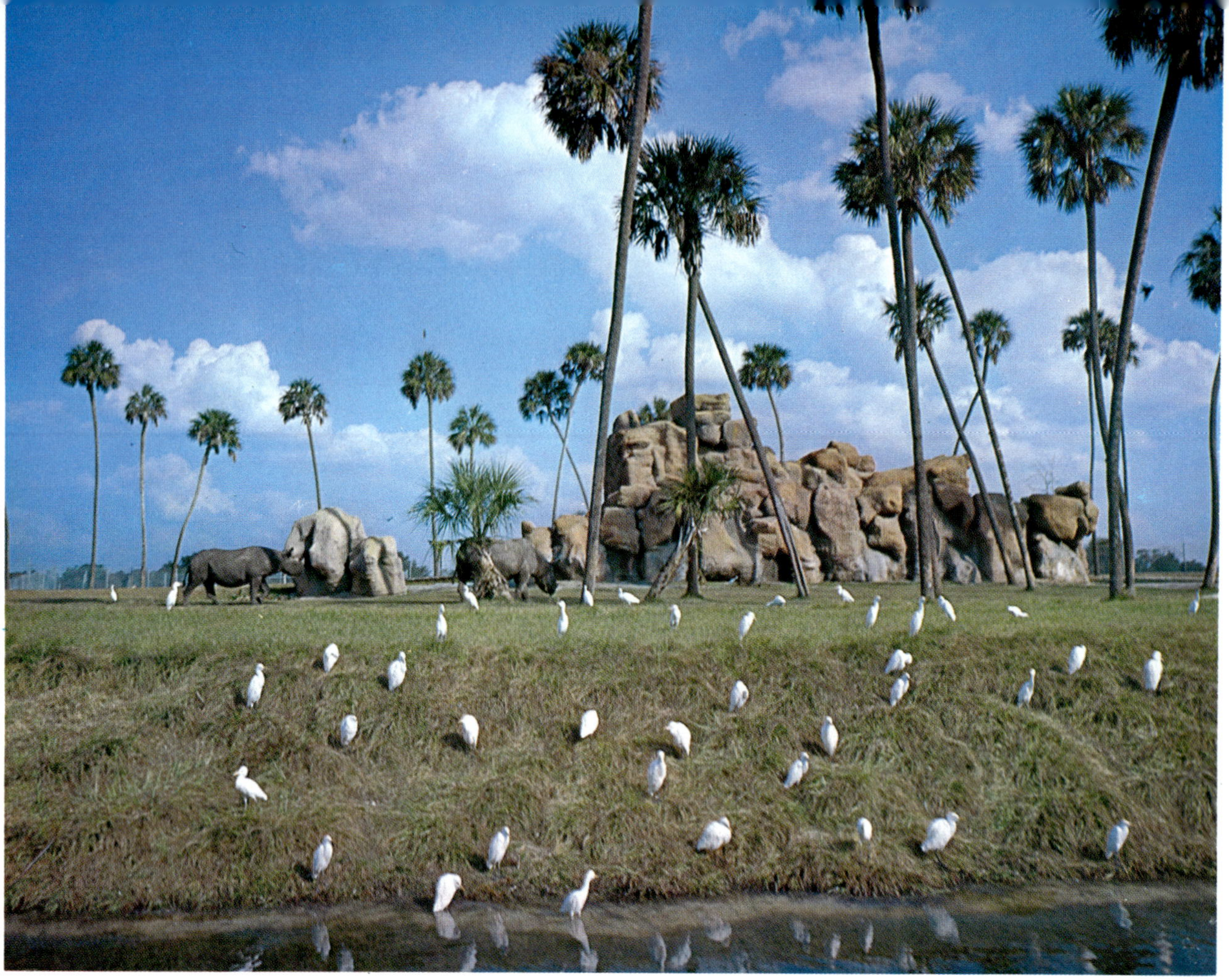

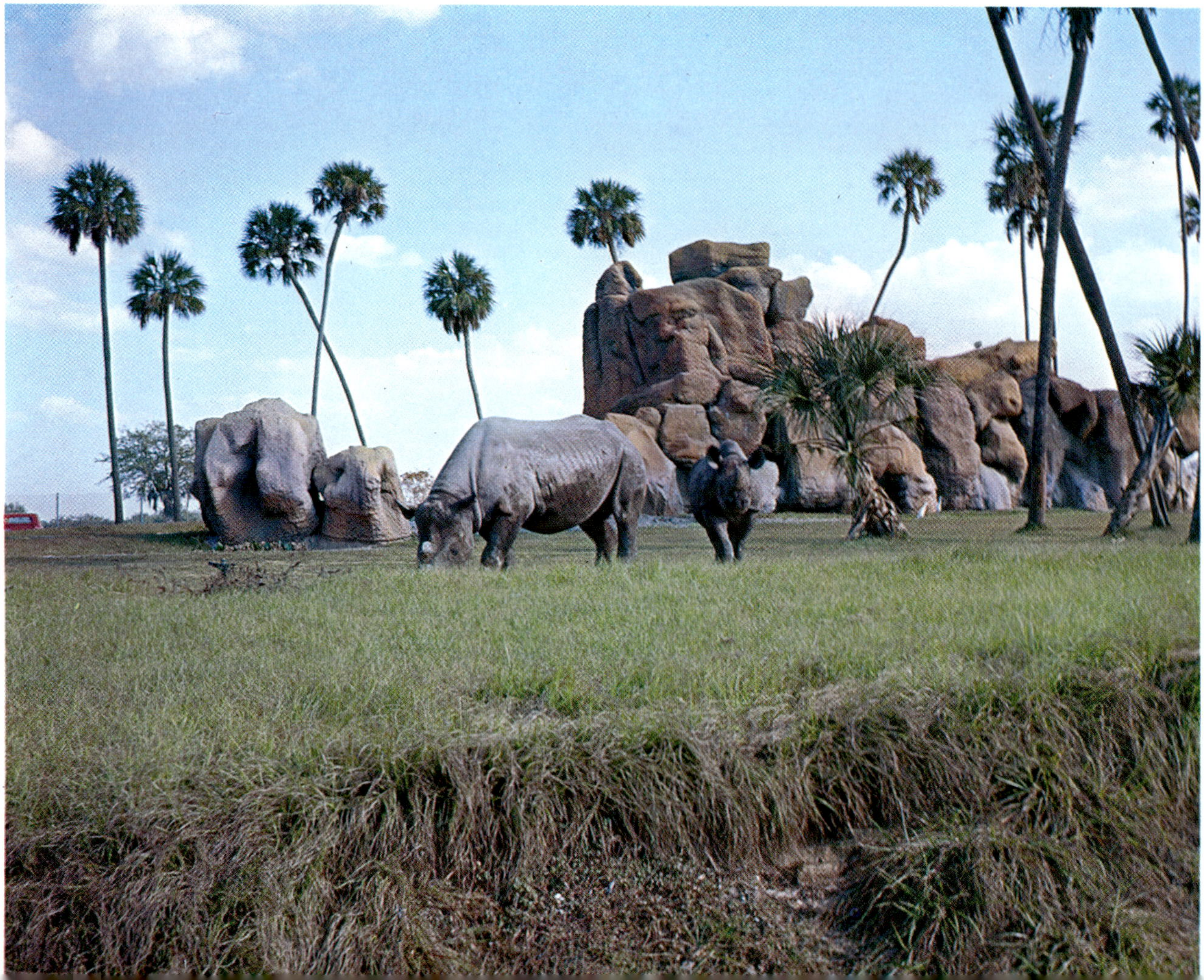

The inhabitants of Busch Gardens in Tampa include flamingos, *above*, rhinoceroses, *opposite, bottom*, and African cattle egrets, *opposite, top*.

Overleaf, at a wildlife management are near Punta Gorda, a deer pauses in a palmetto scrub.

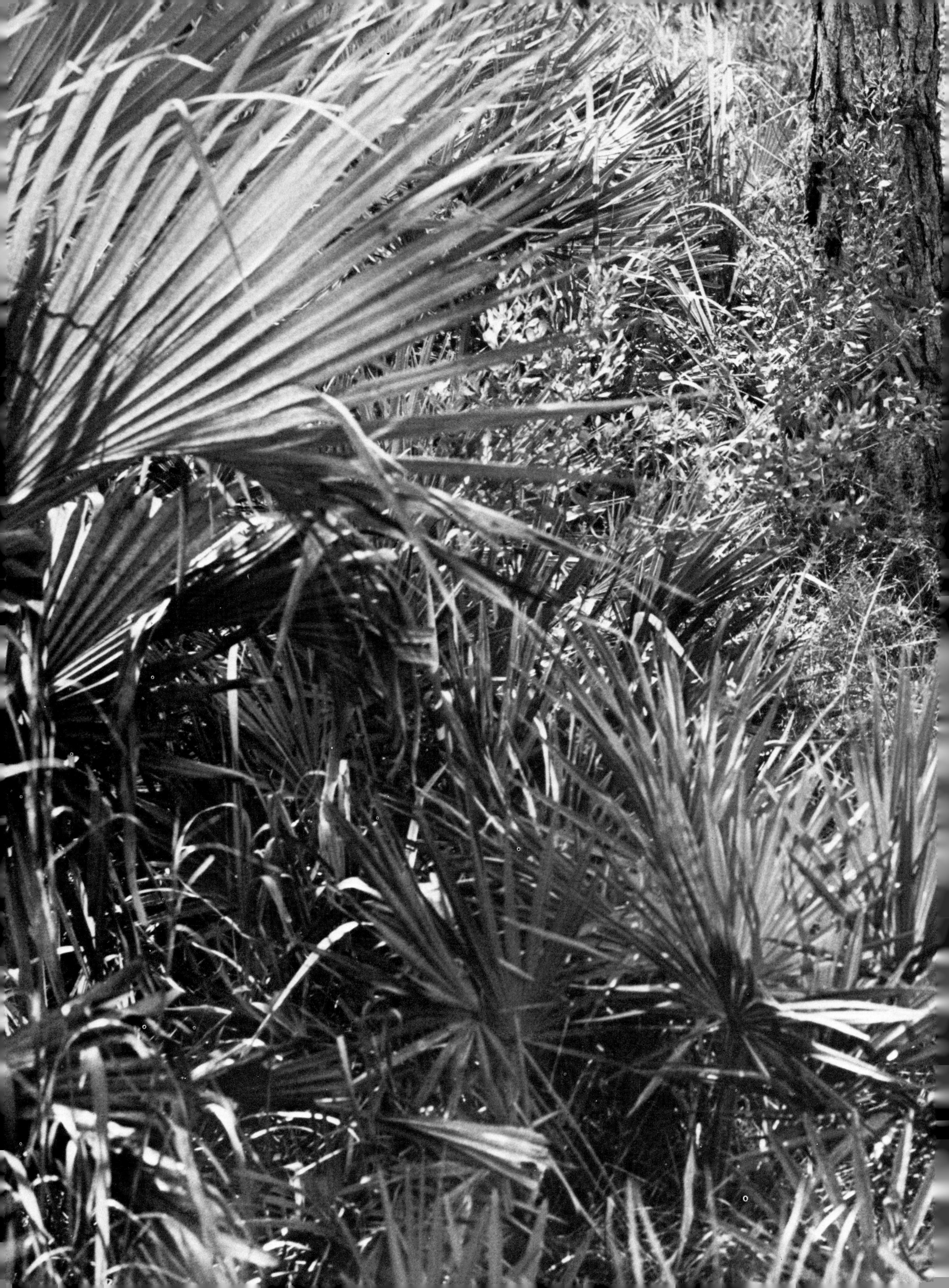

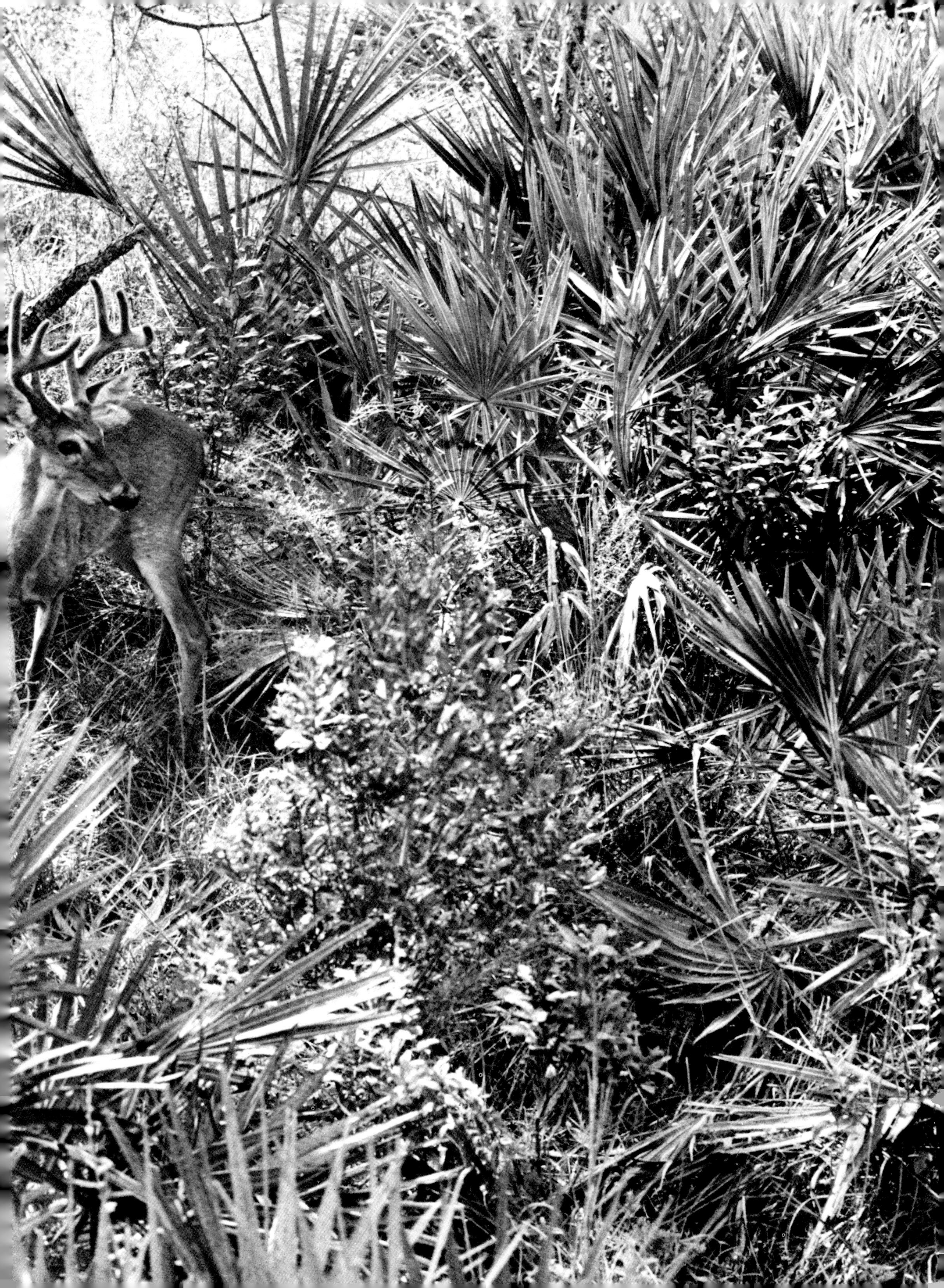

Above, on the Seminole reservation at Brighton, near Lake Okeechobee, an Indian cowboy watches over his herd. *Opposite,* the Peace River, which flows through Southwest Florida to empty into the Gulf of Mexico.

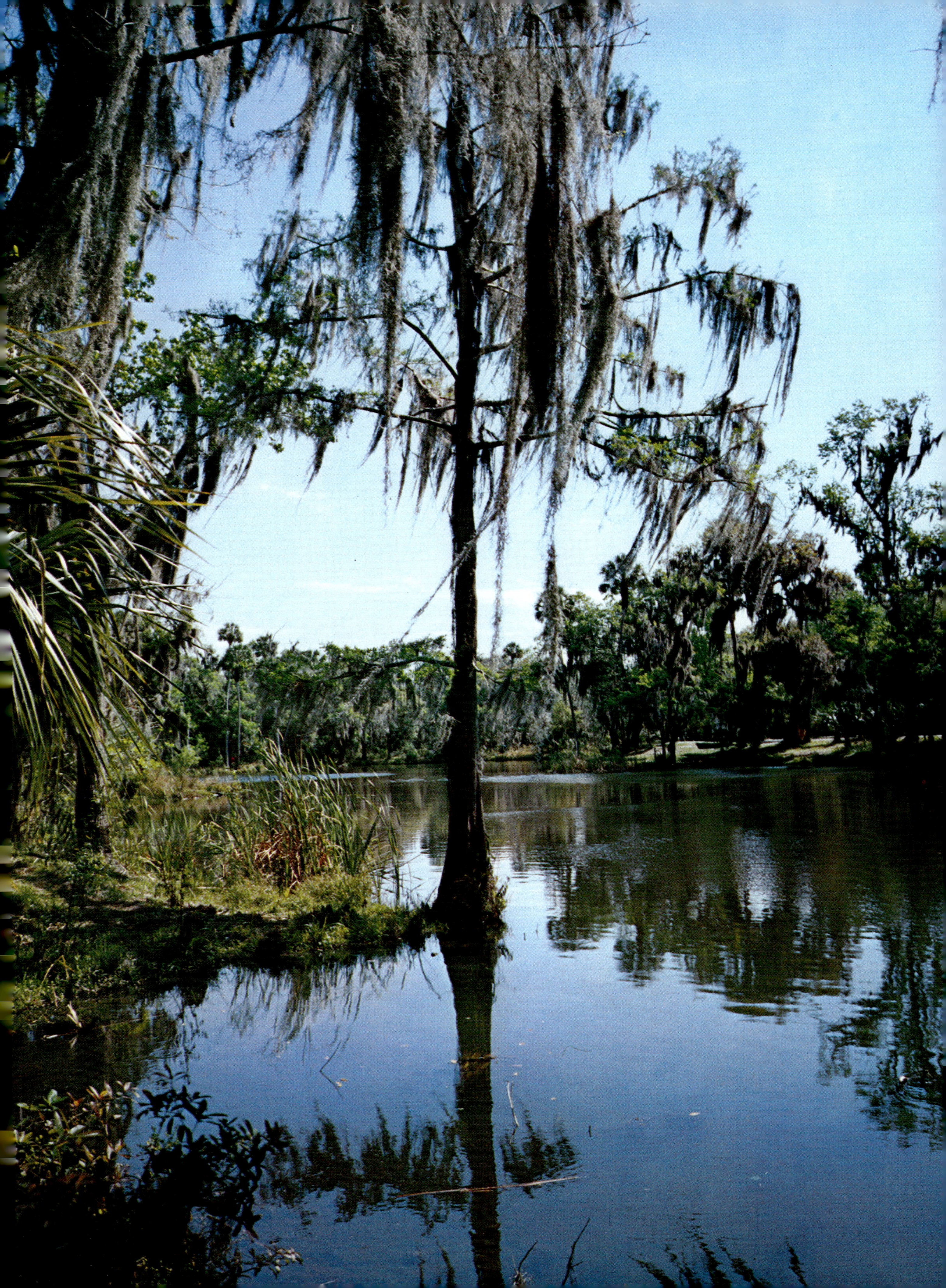

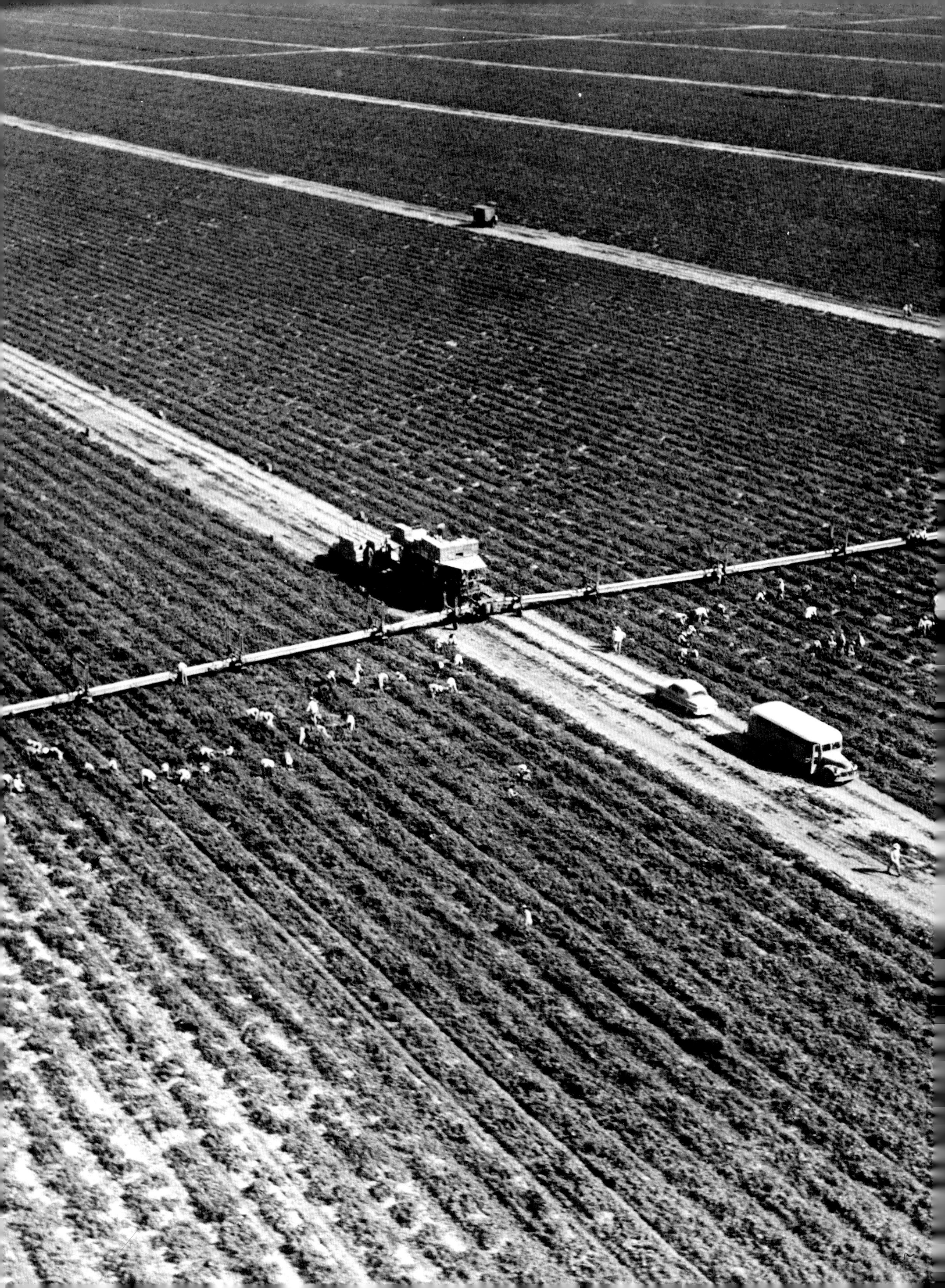

Opposite, a long-armed conveyor, on which the crop is graded and packed, is driven across a field of tomatoes at Princeton, a few miles outside Miami. *Below*, a lock on one of the many canals that flow out of Lake Okeechobee.

Below, the skyline of West Palm Beach. *At right*, the Kennedy mansion at Palm Beach. *Opposite*, a windy day on the Palm Beach oceanfront.

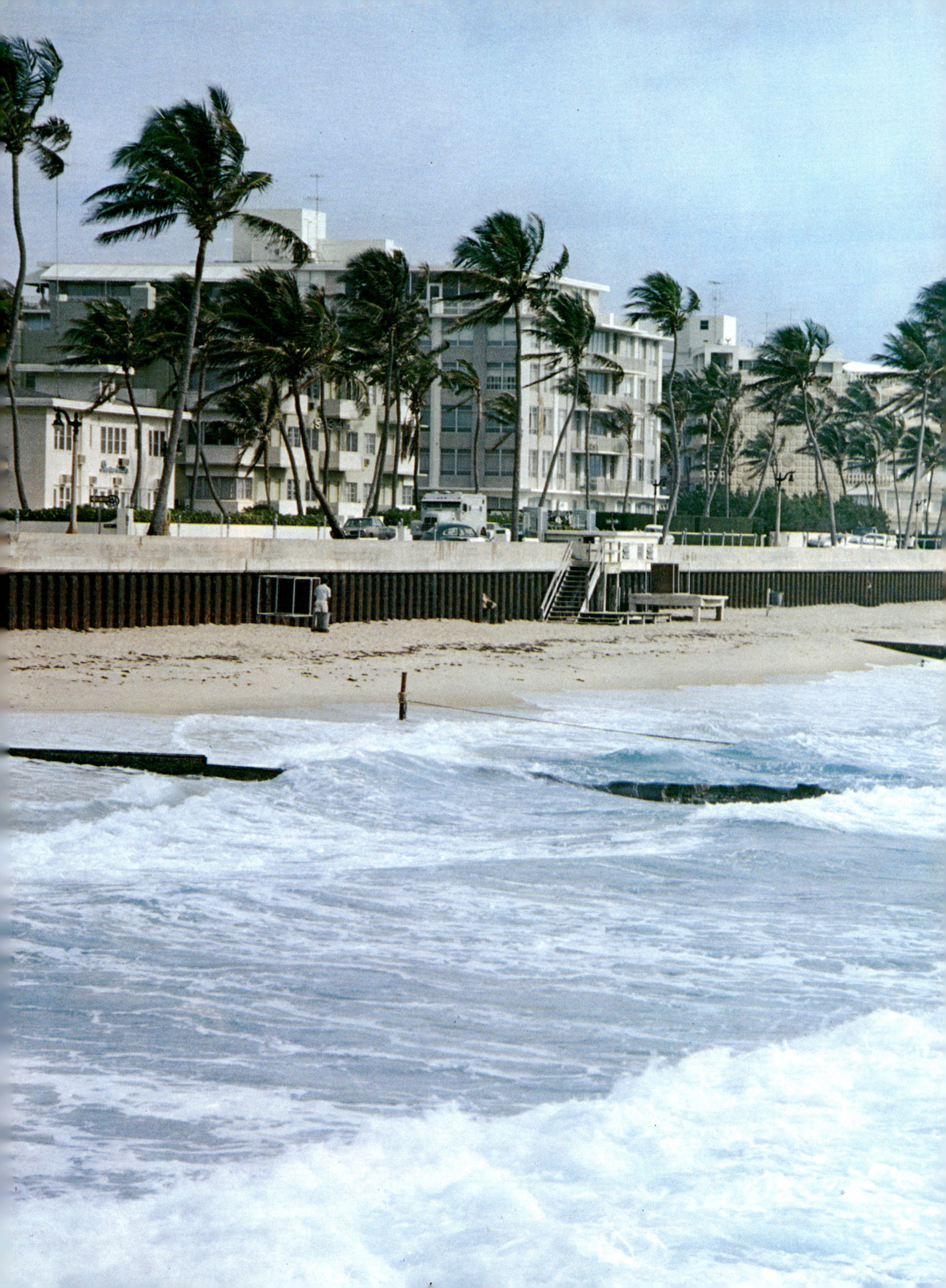

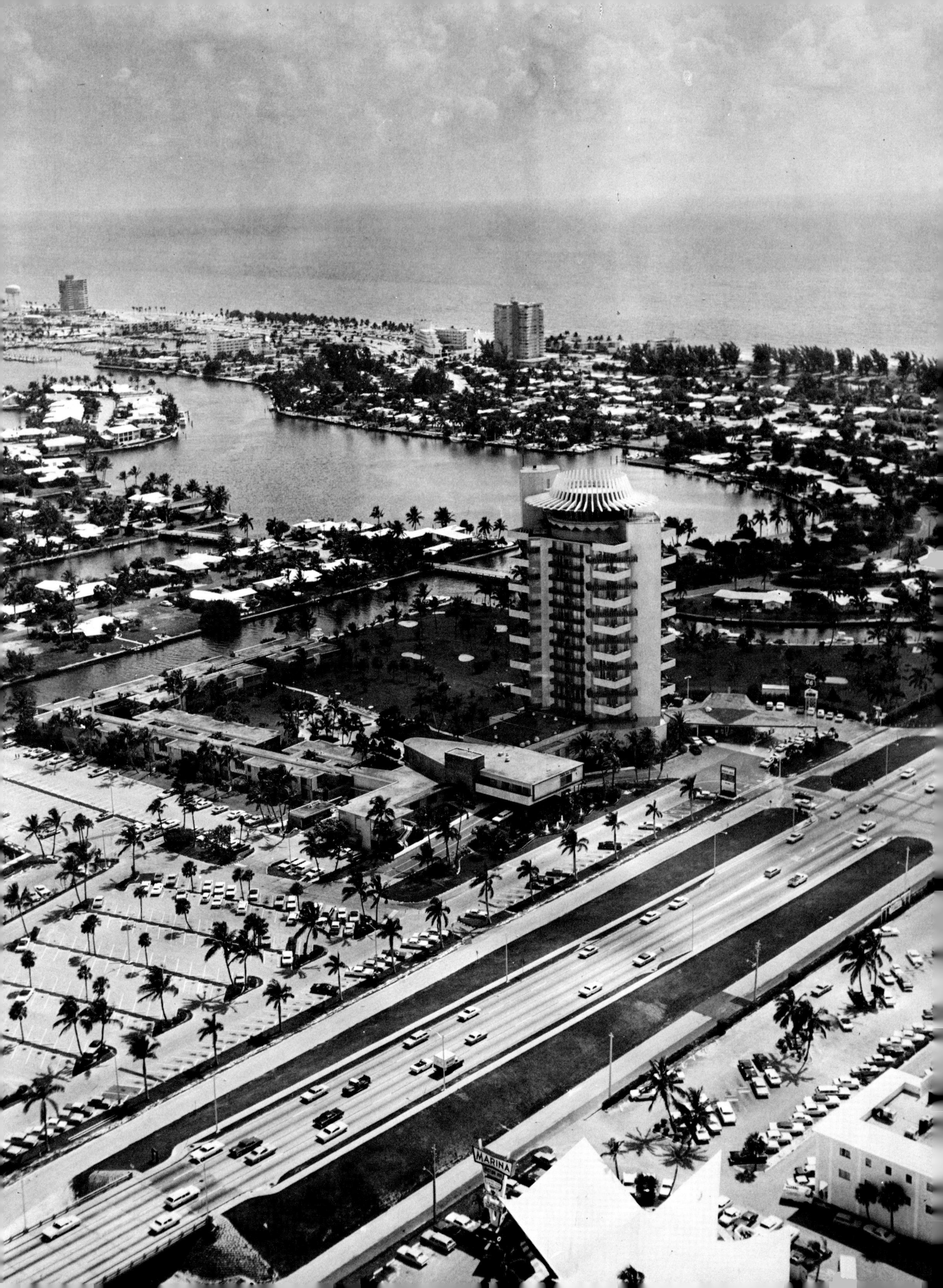
MARINA

At Fort Lauderdale: *below*, palm trees on the beach; *at left*, a sternwheeler on the Intracoastal Waterway. *Opposite*, Fort Lauderdale beach, with one of the broad boulevards leading to it.

Overleaf: The luxurious Flagler mansion in Palm Beach is now a museum.

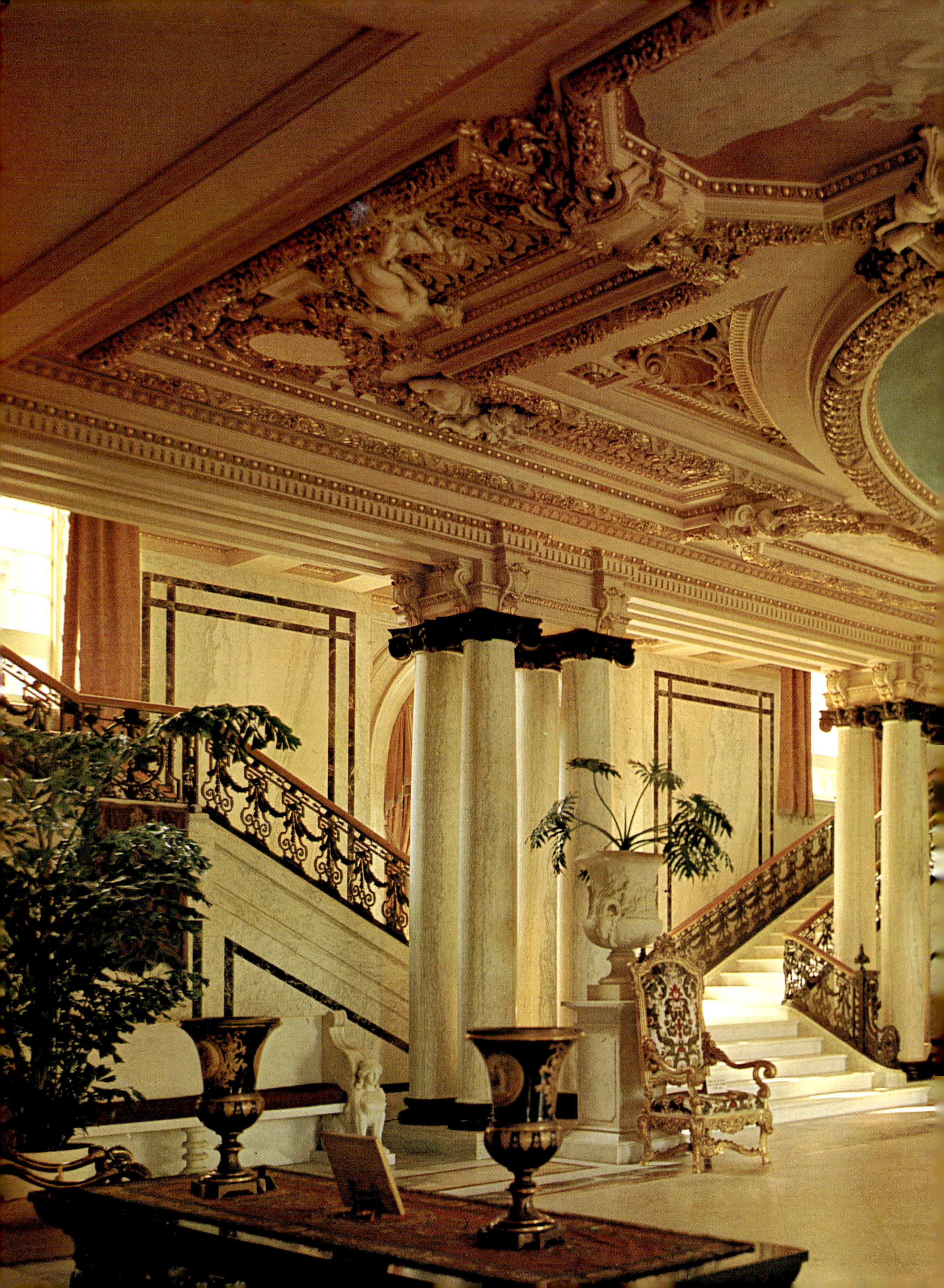

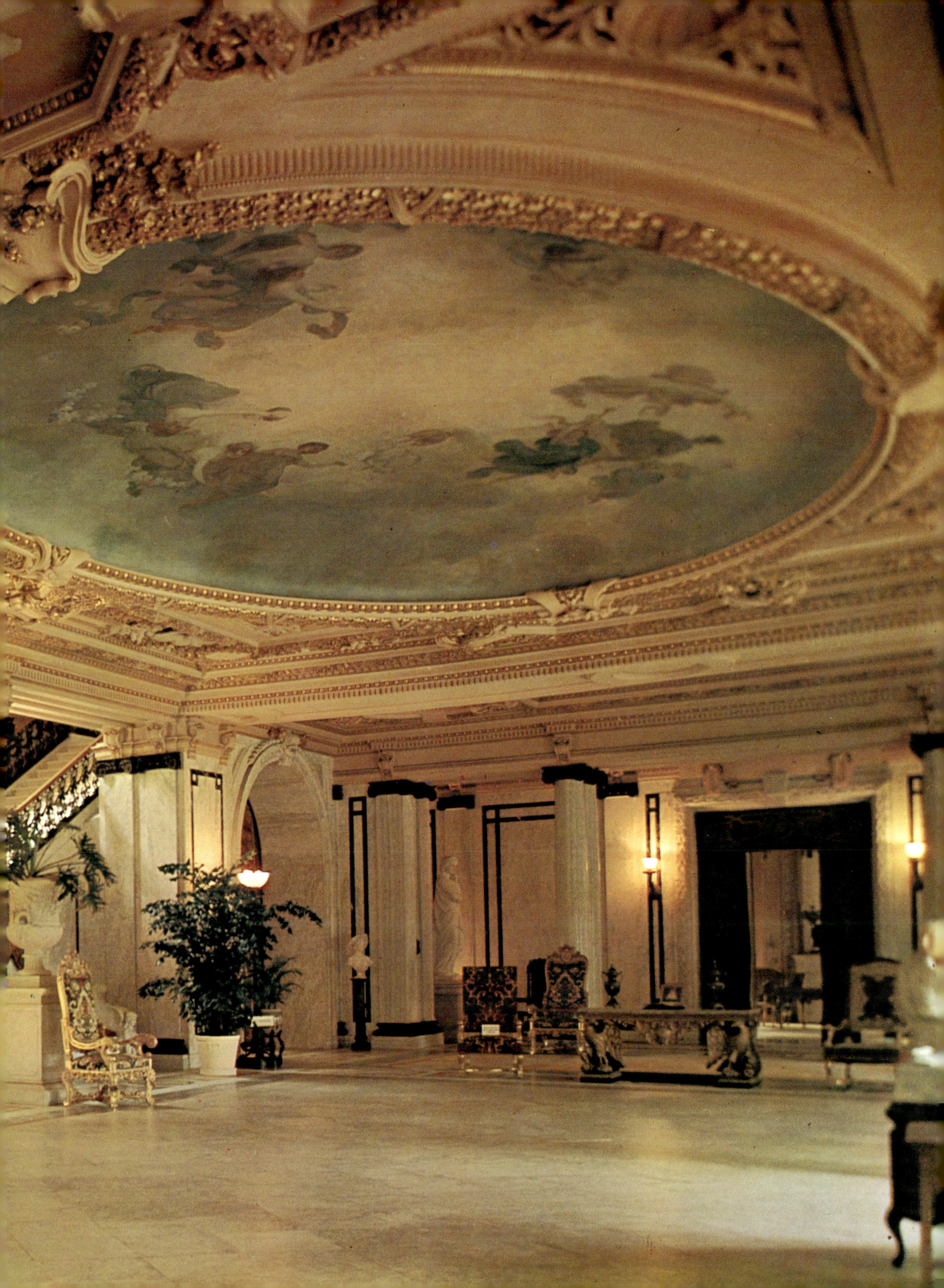

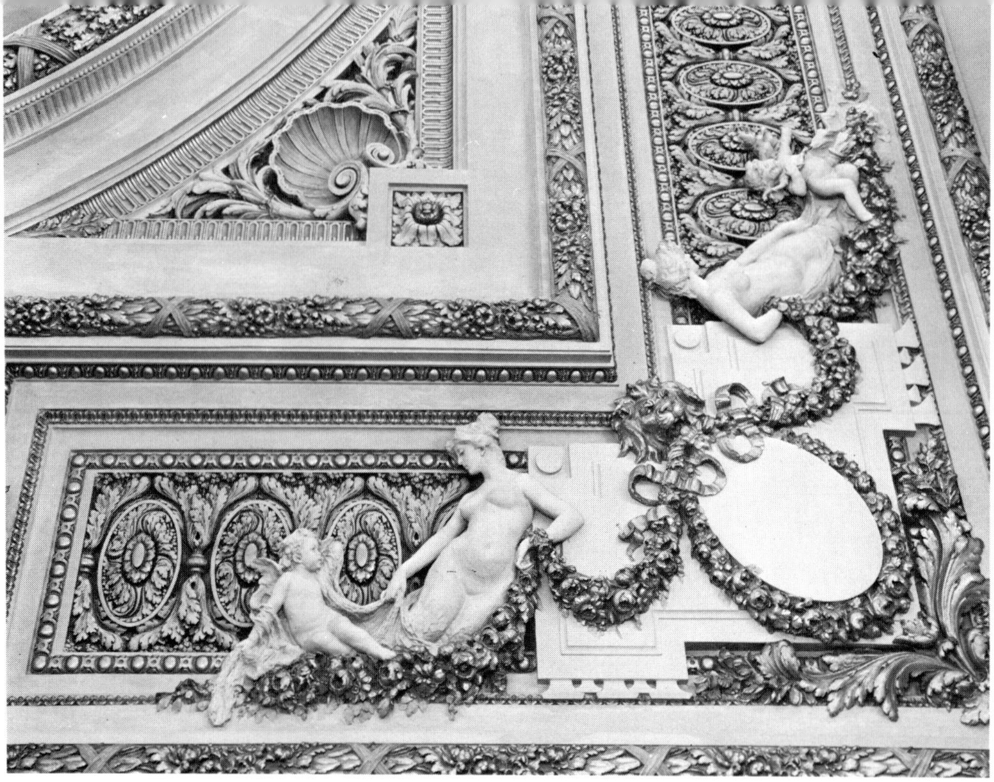

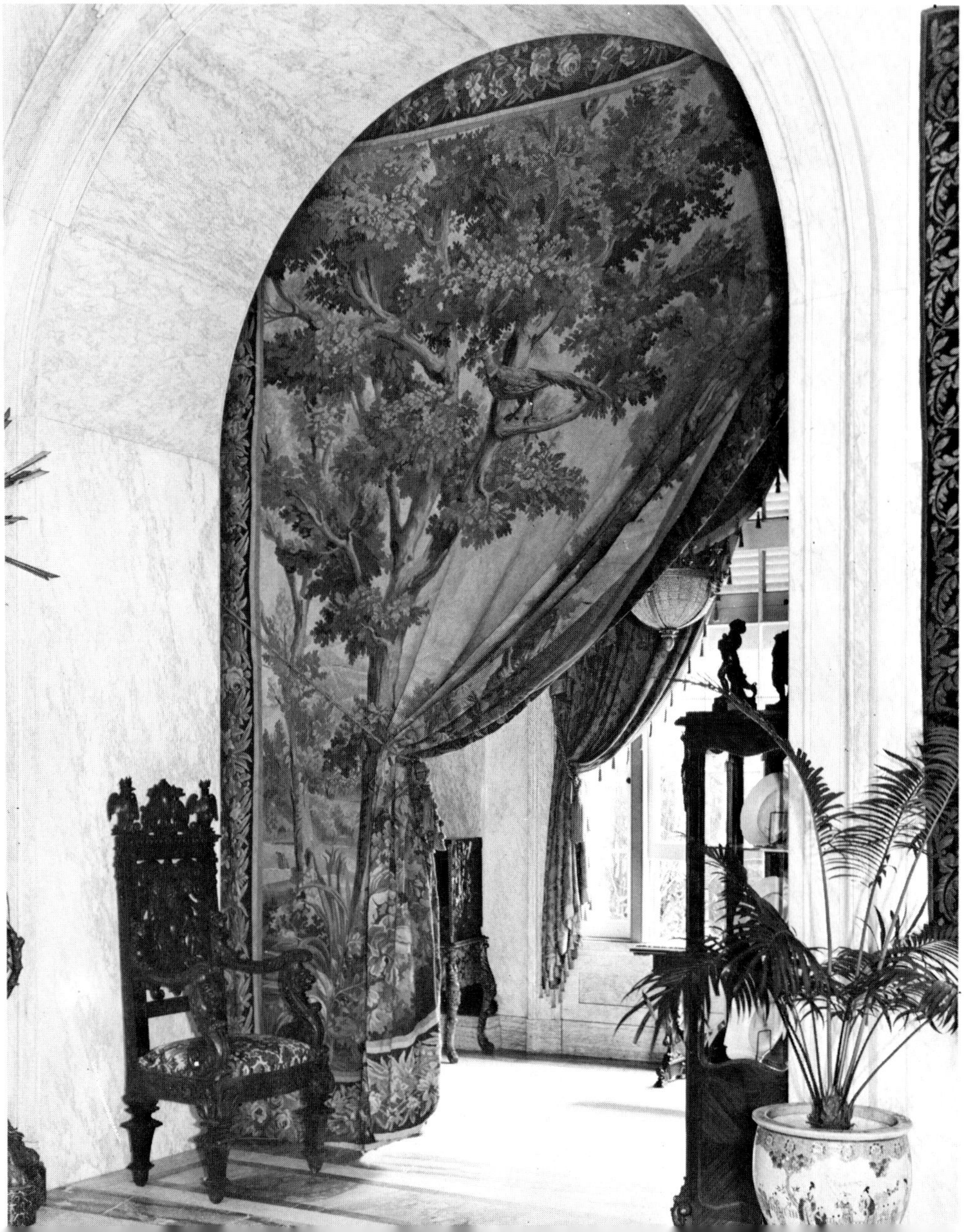

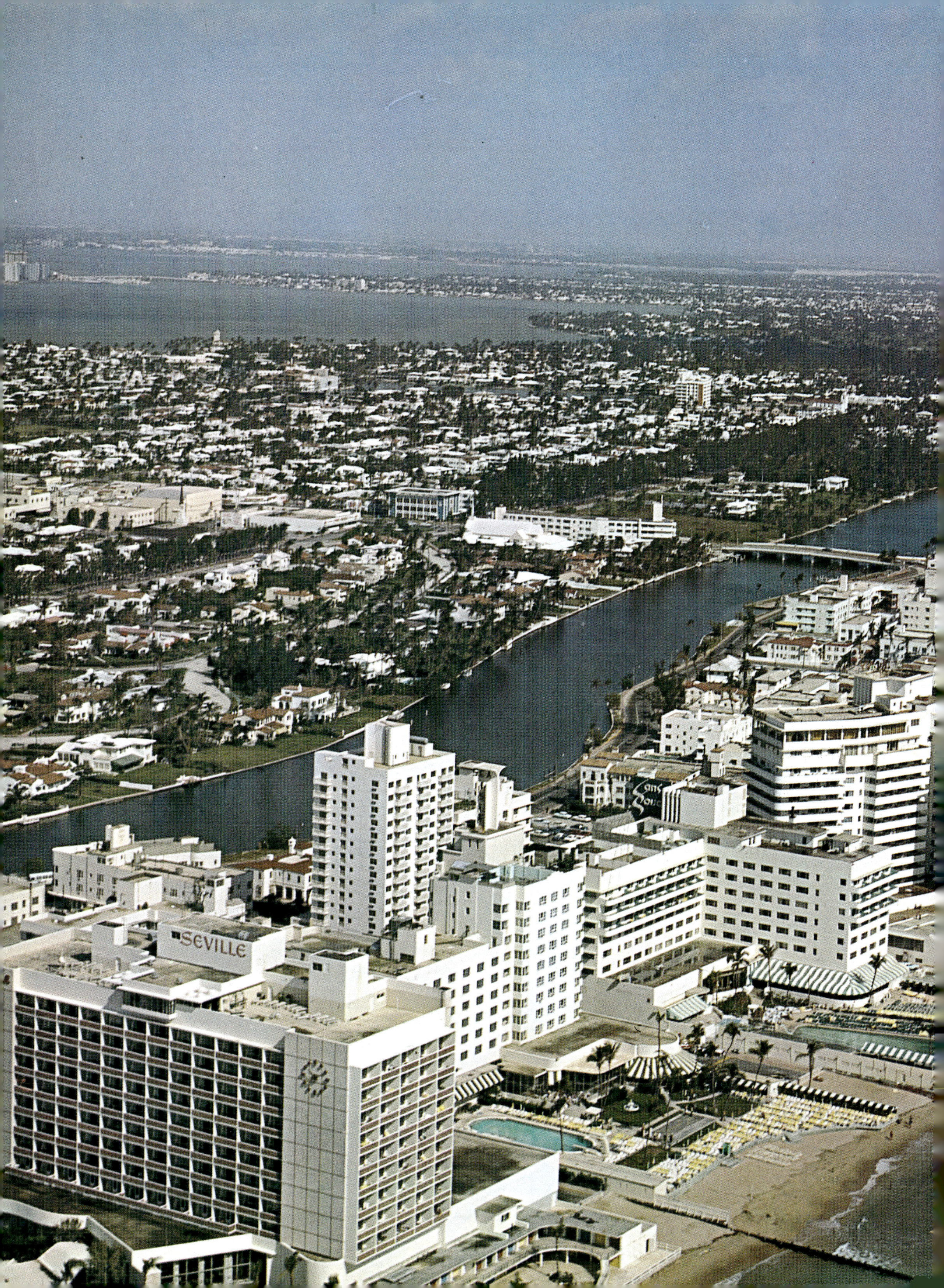
SEVILLE

Lavish decoration has always been a hallmark of Florida's Gold Coast. *Opposite*, two details from the Flagler mansion, built in 1901. On this page details from Miami Beach's Doral Beach Hotel which opened in 1962.

Overleaf: The luxury hotels of Miami Beach.

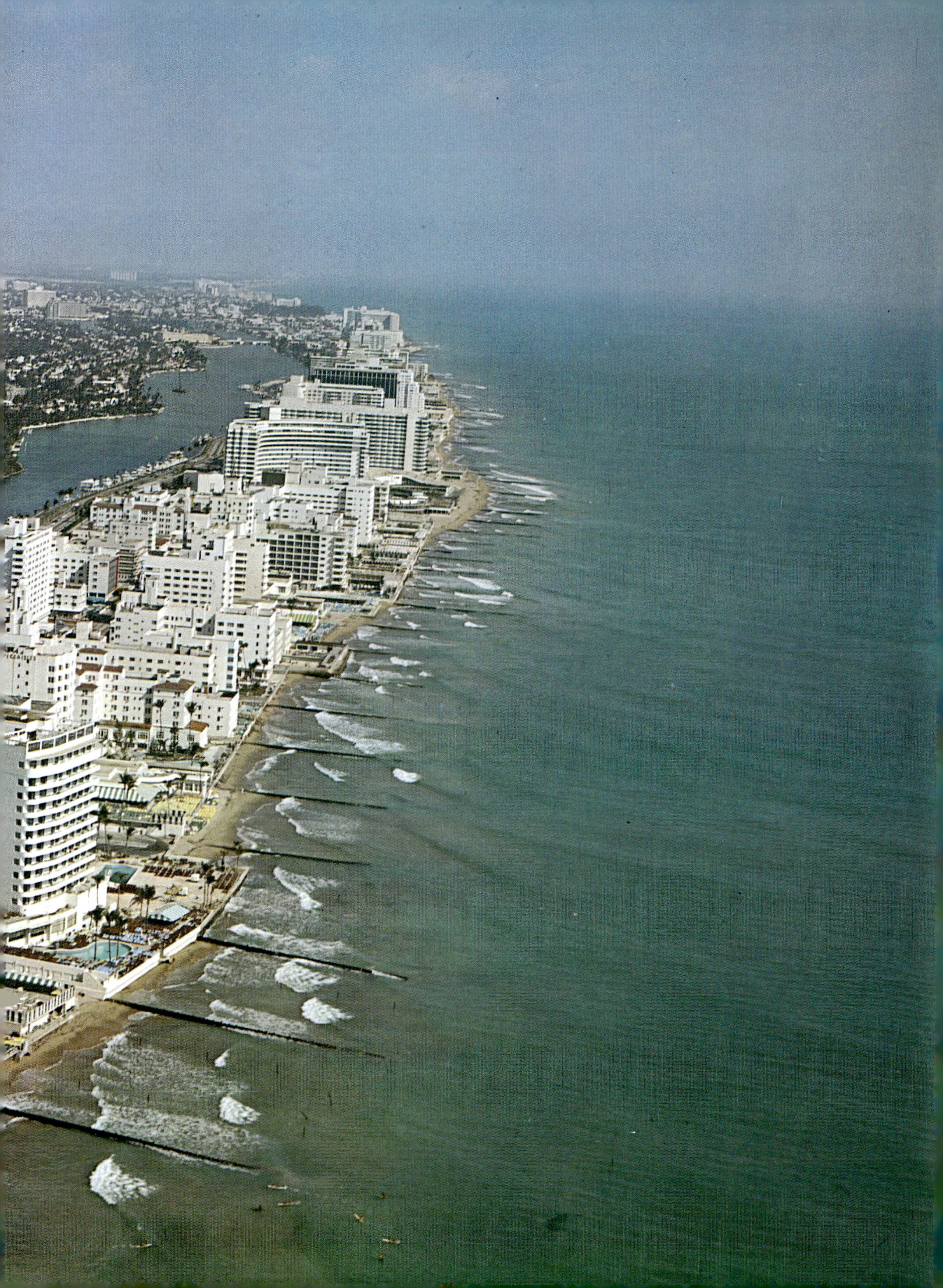

At Miami: *top*, the skyscrapers of downtown Miami, overlooking a marina. *Above*, pelicans at a Miami pier (*left*) and parrots at Parrot Jungle. *Opposite*, a thatch palm at Fairchild Tropical Gardens.

Overleaf: The hotels of Miami Beach are visible in the distance beyond the islands that dot the peaceful waters of Biscayne Bay.

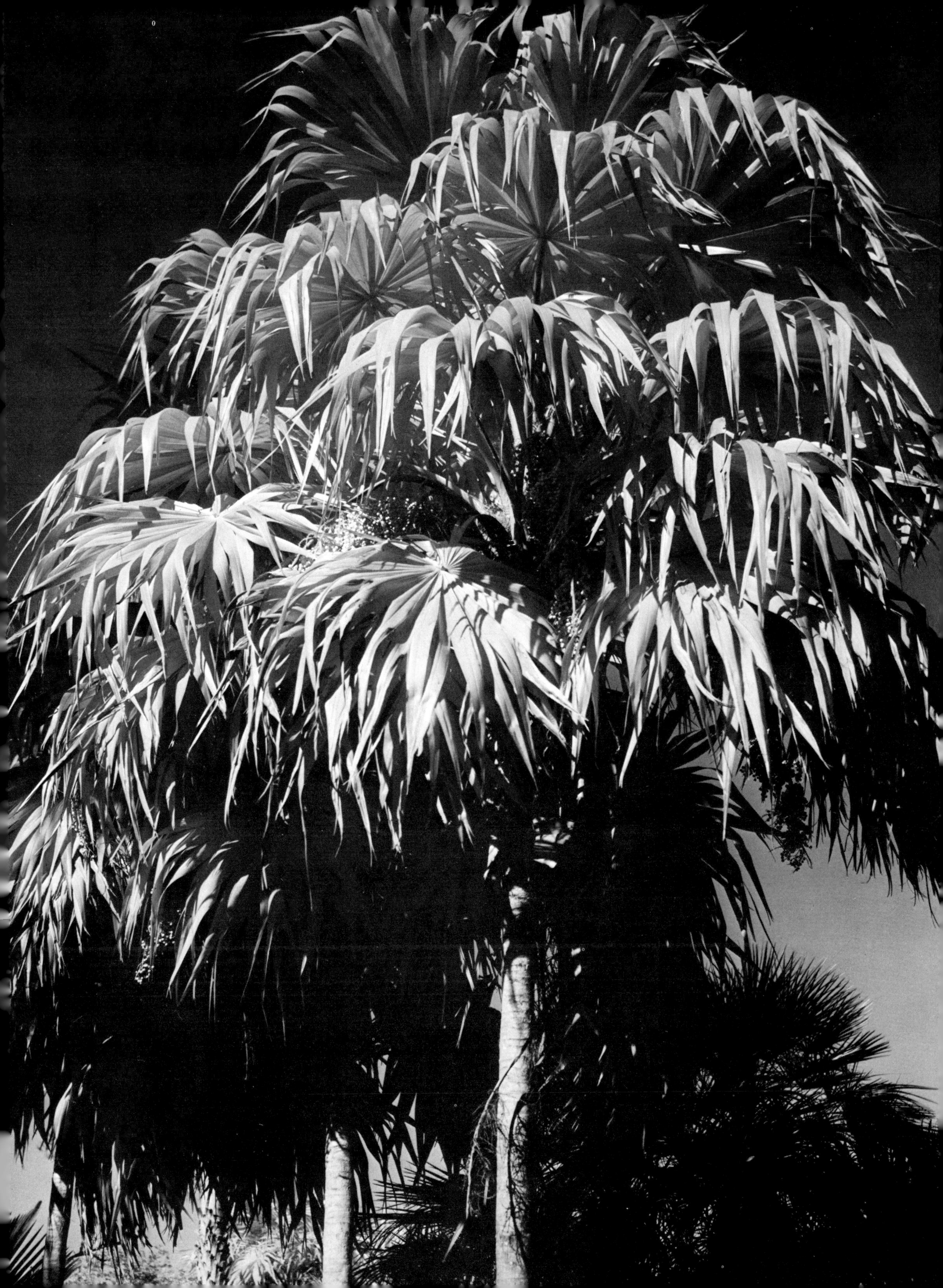

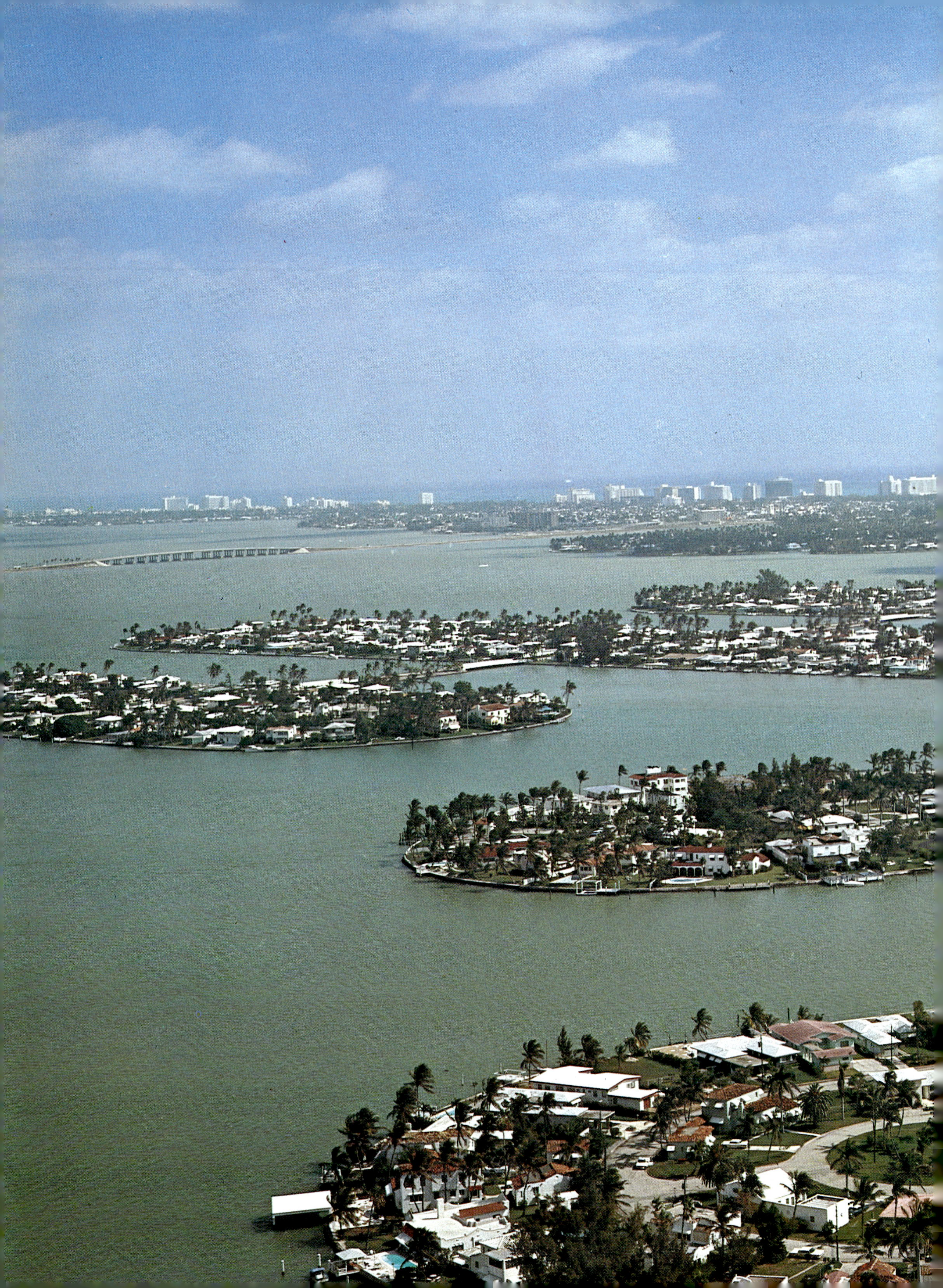

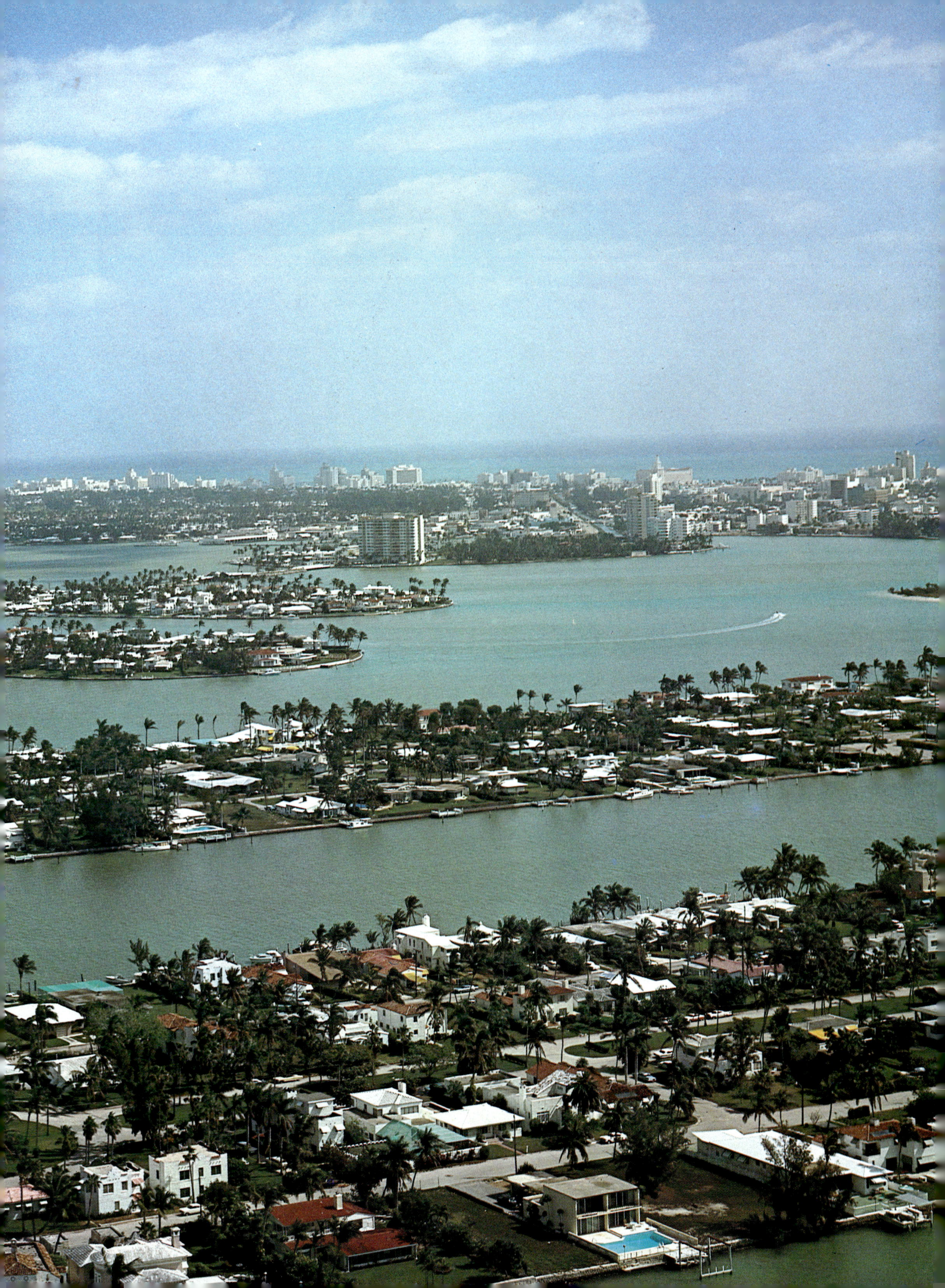

Above, a breakwater in the form of a stone barge lies offshore at the Villa Vizcaya Museum in Miami. *Opposite* is another Miami art monument, the eleventh-century Spanish cloisters of St. Bernard's Monastery in North Miami Beach. *At right* is a statue from the cloisters, of the Spanish King, Alfonso VIII.

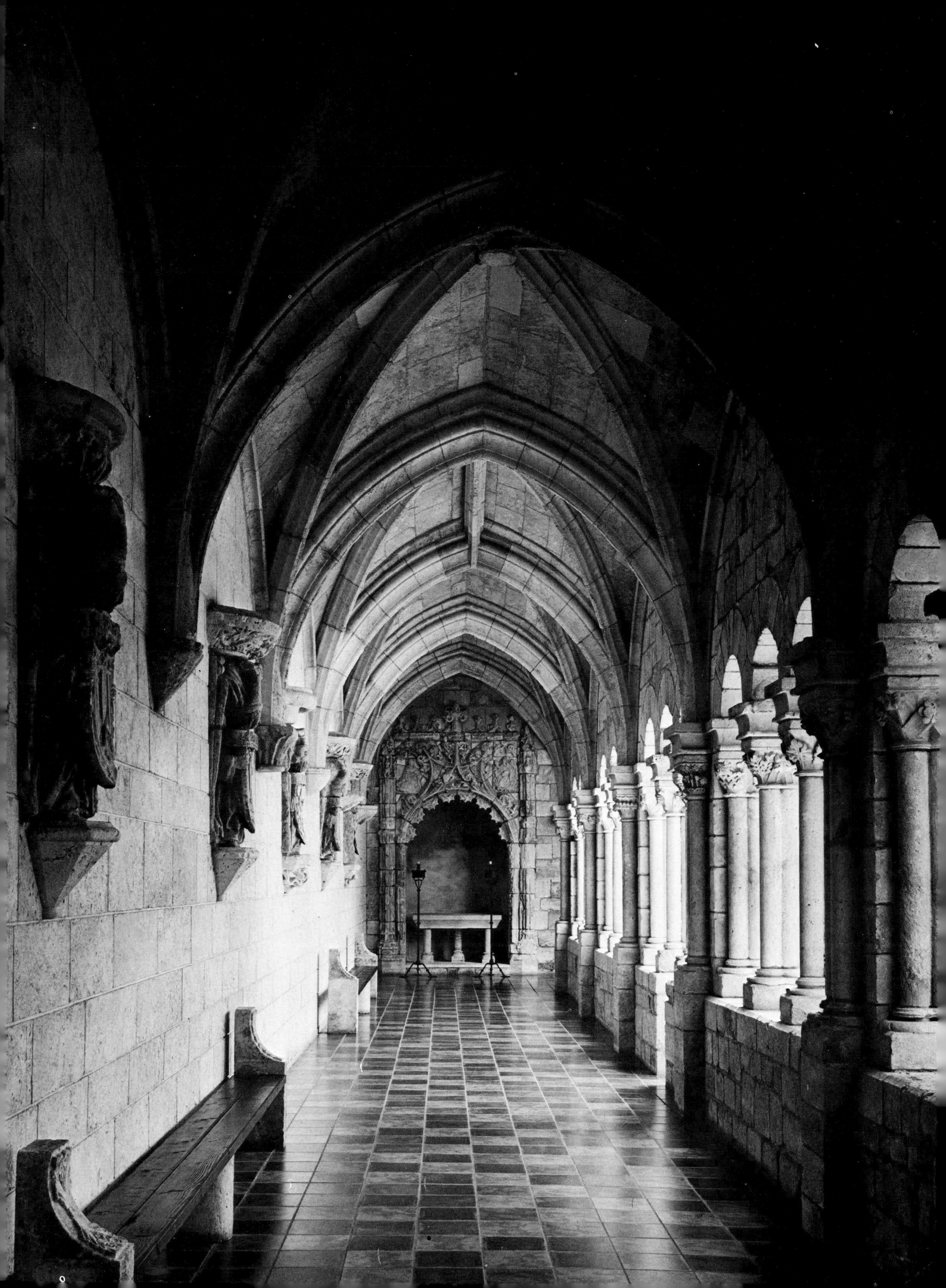

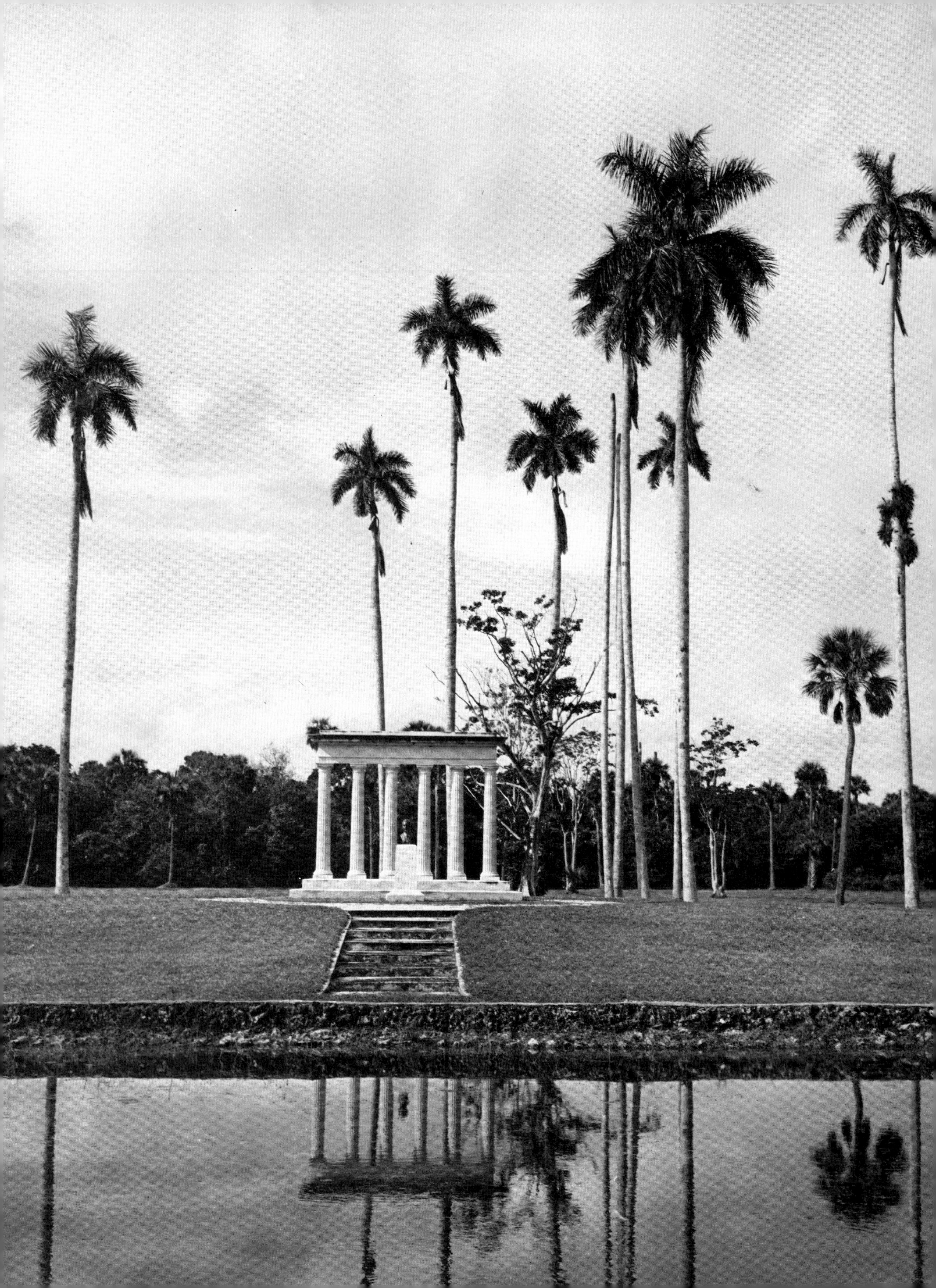

Collier-Seminole State Park, *opposite*, stands in the southwest Florida region where the Seminoles fled for refuge after the government ordered them to leave the state in 1836. *Below*, lily pads in Corkscrew Swamp Sanctuary, which contains the country's largest stand of virgin bald cypresses.

Overleaf: the cypresses of Corkscrew Swamp.

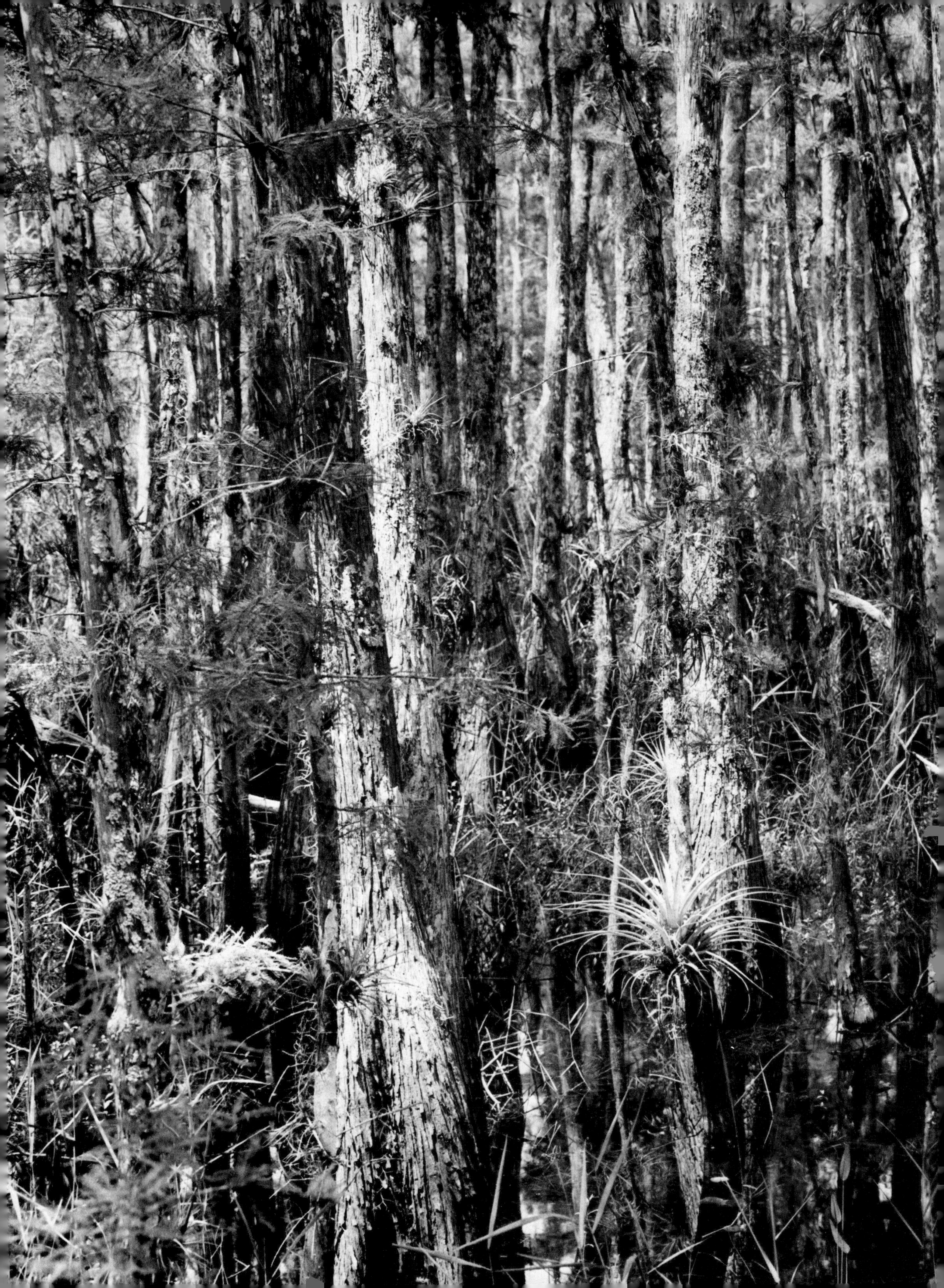

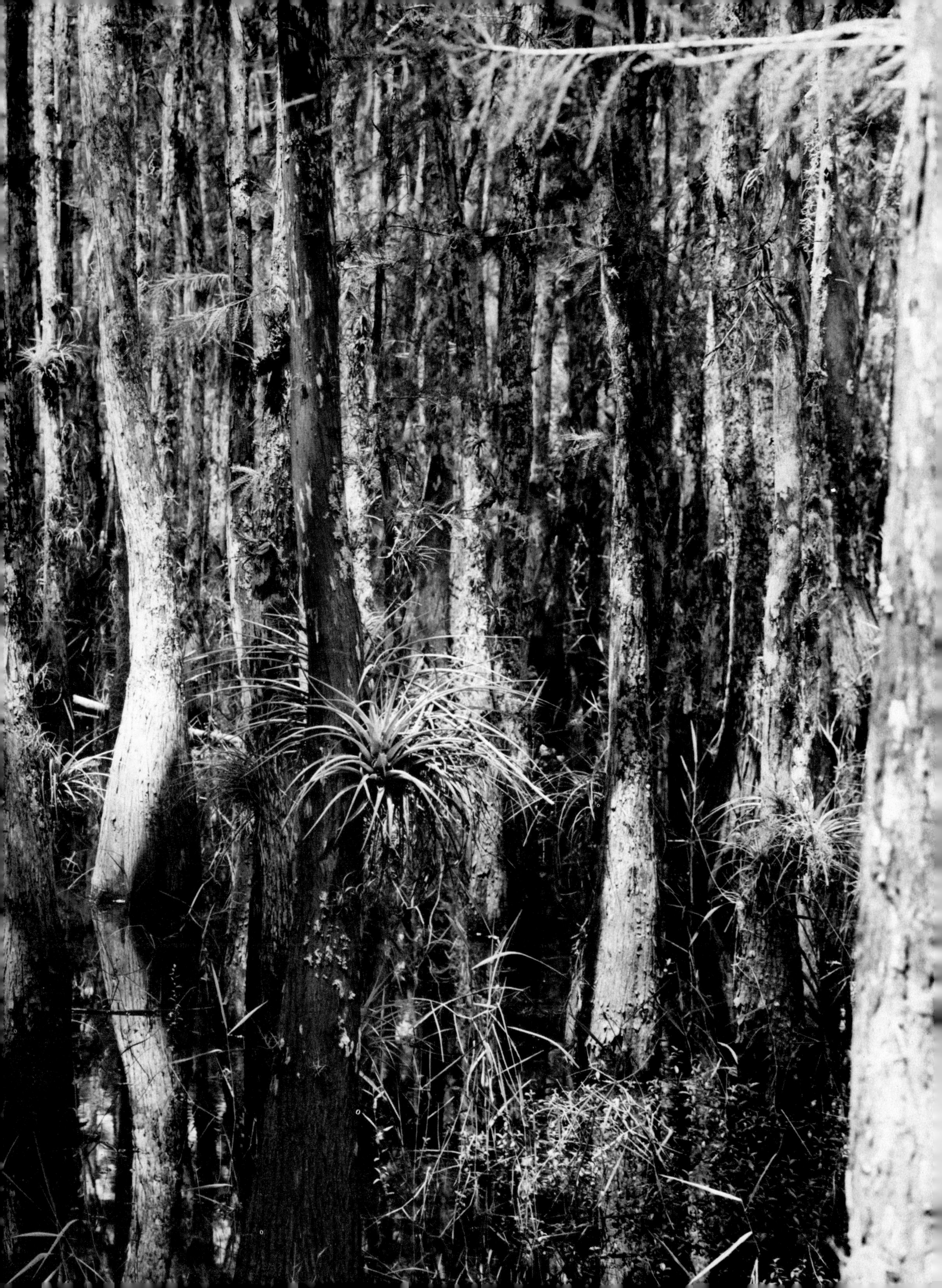

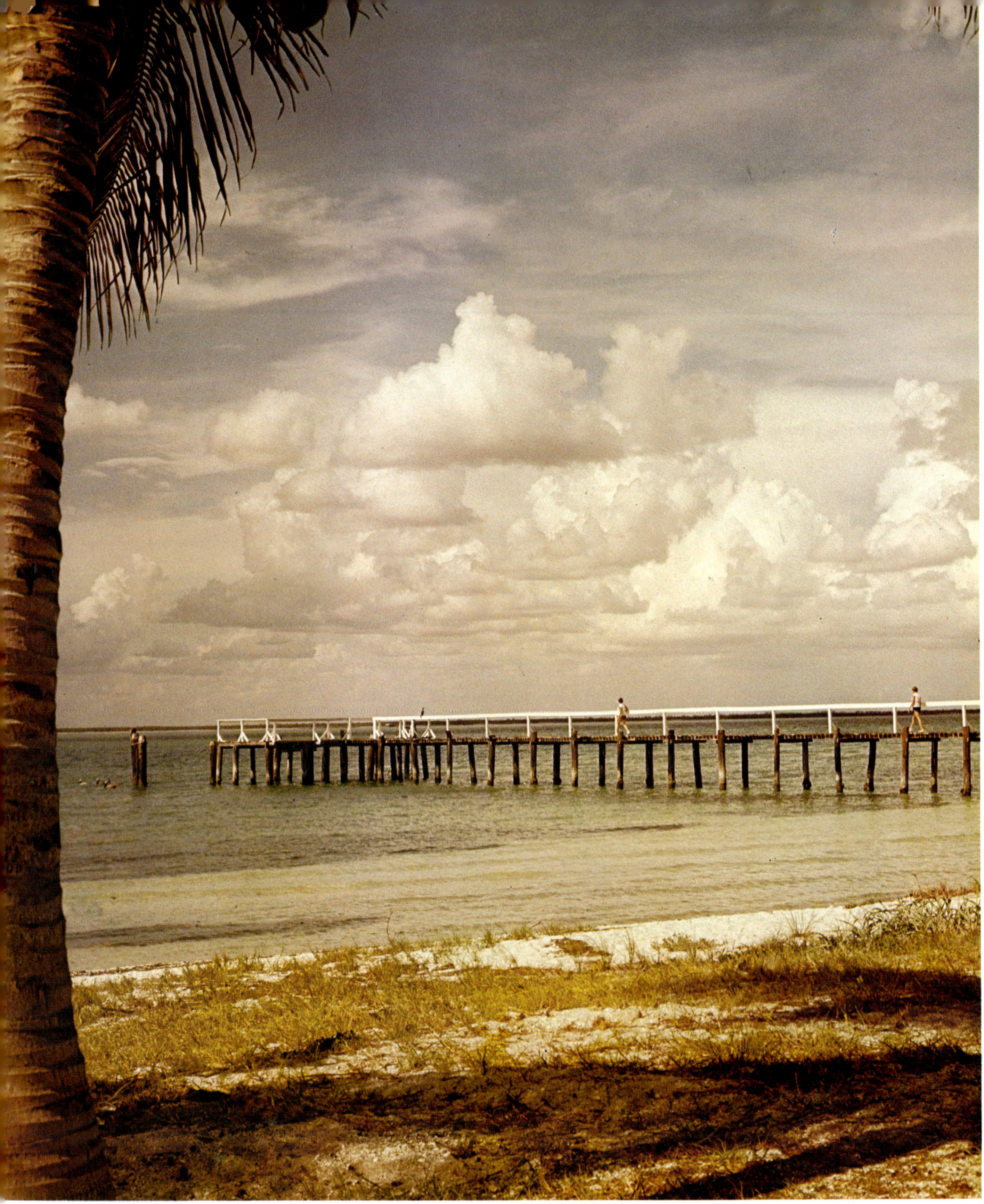

Mangrove swamps cover the Ten Thousand Islands, *above*, just north of
Everglades National Park. A shifting mass of mangrove swampland, the islands
were not fully charted until 1970. *Opposite,* the fishing pier at Sanibel Island.

Above, fishnets dry in the sun at Marco Island. *Opposite,* the "Boulevard of Palms" in Fort Myers, the major city of the southwest coastal region.

141

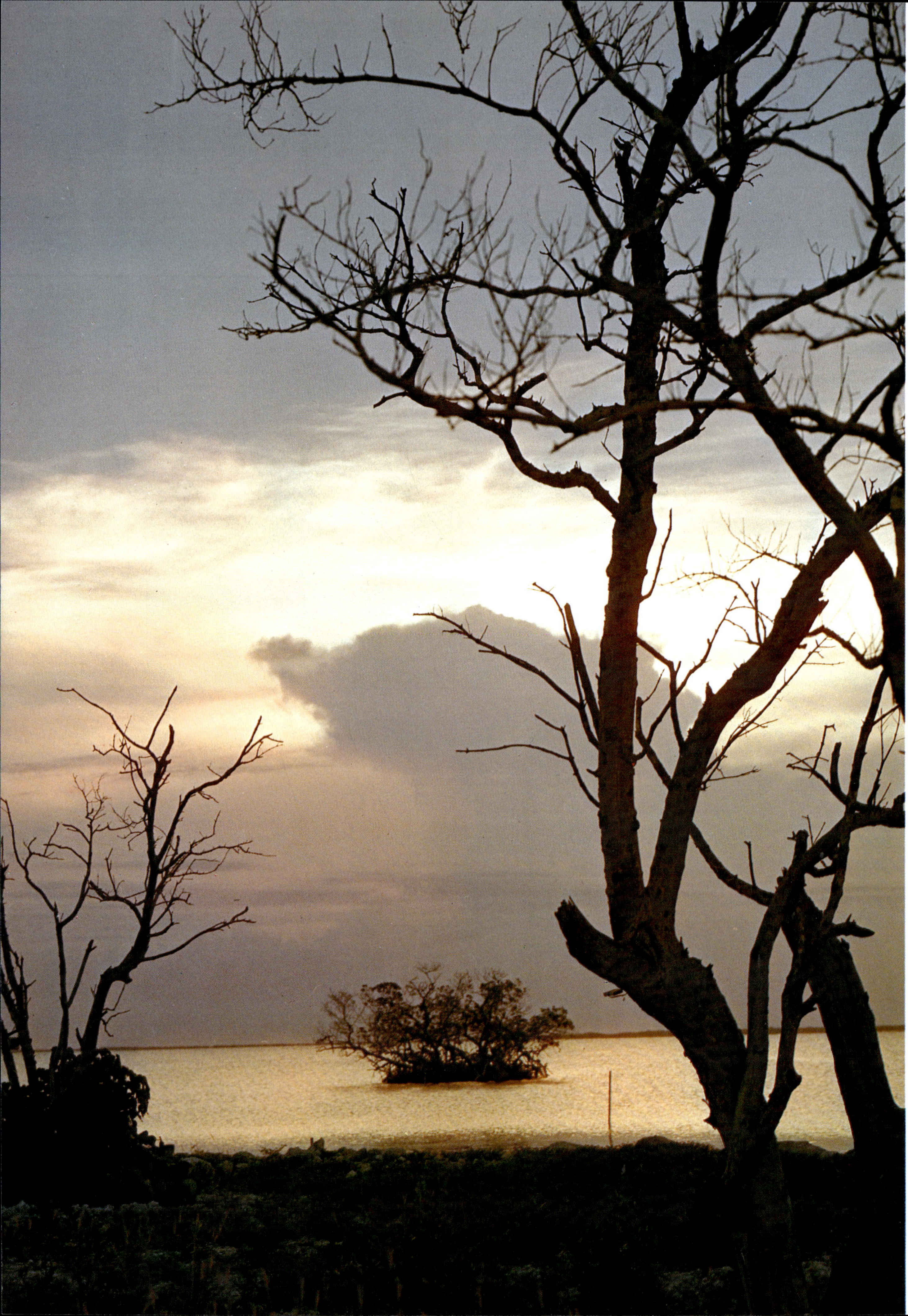

Above, along the Tamiami trail at the northern edge of Everglades National Park.
Opposite, a coastal sunset in the Everglades.

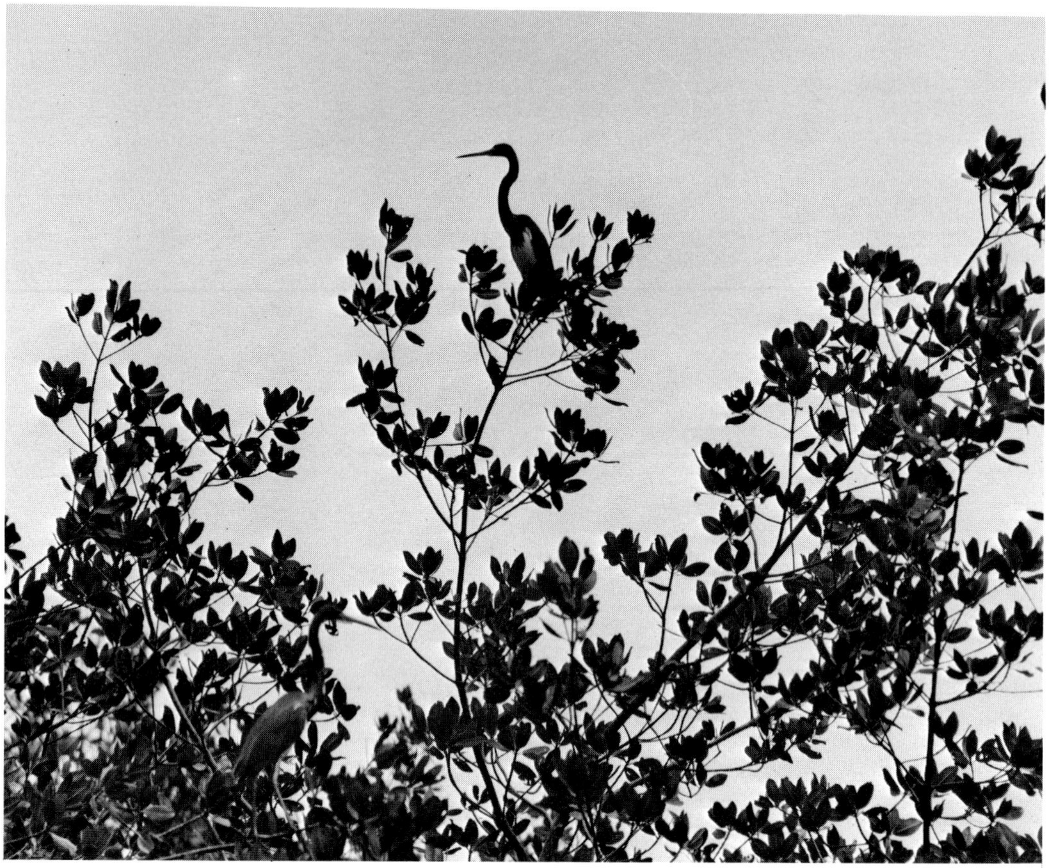

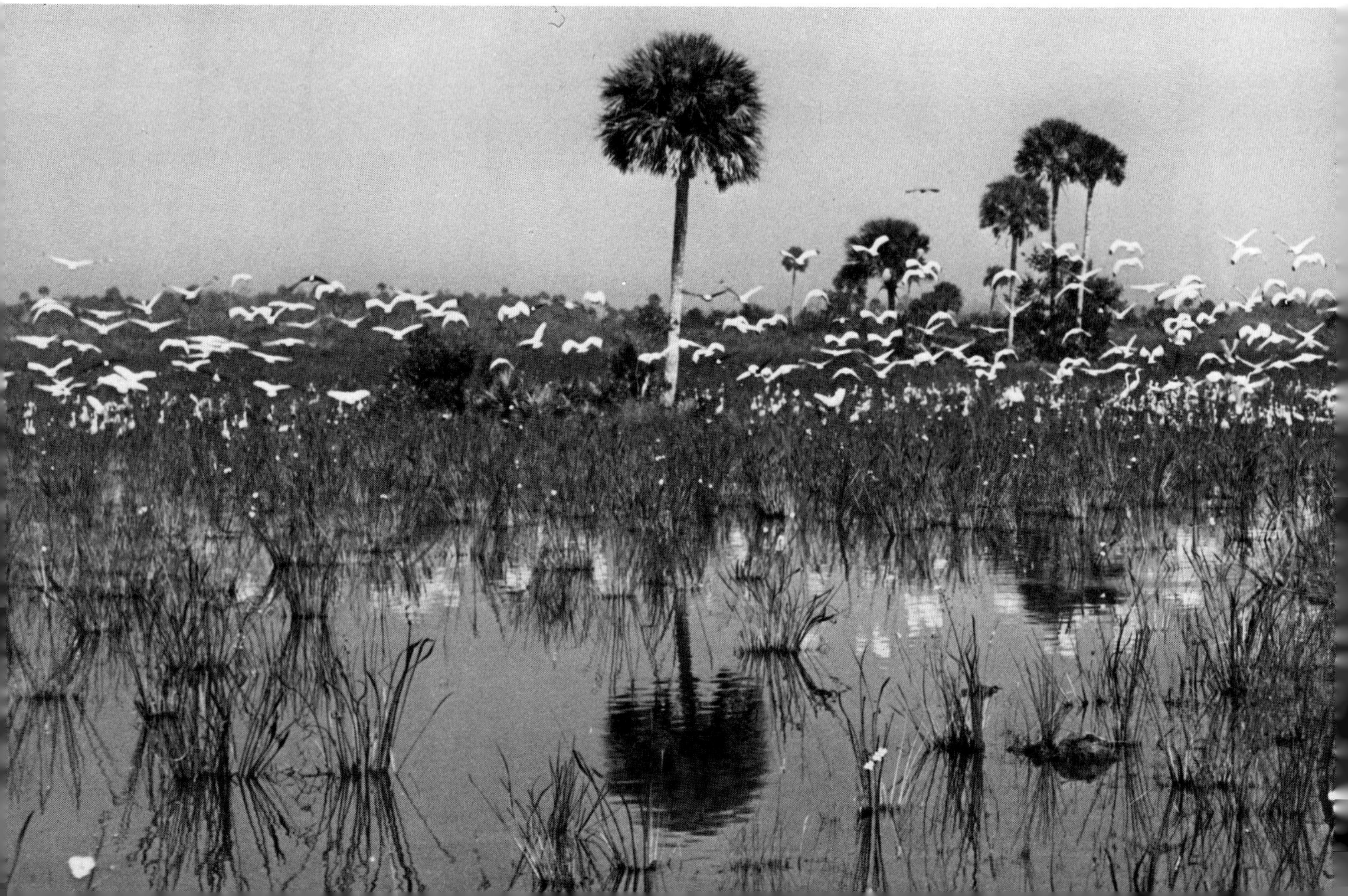

Bird life in the Everglades: *below*, a flock of white ibis; *at right*, frigate birds at Tern Key; *opposite*, Louisiana heron.

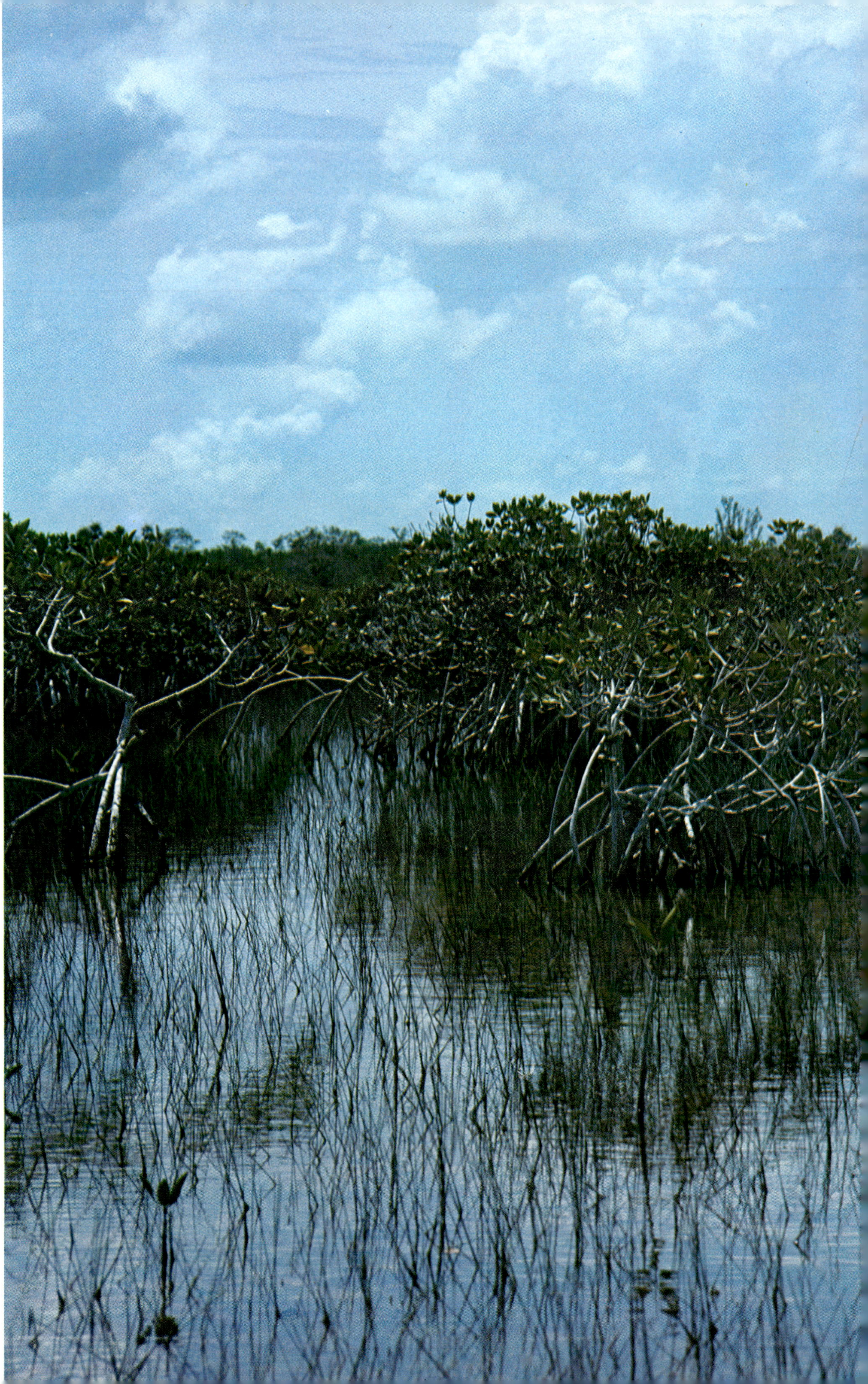

An impenetrable
Everglades thicket,
typical of the landscape
in the National Park.

Off Key Largo lies John Pennekamp Coral Reef State Park, with its intricate coral formations, *below,* and its brightly colored tropical fish, *opposite.*

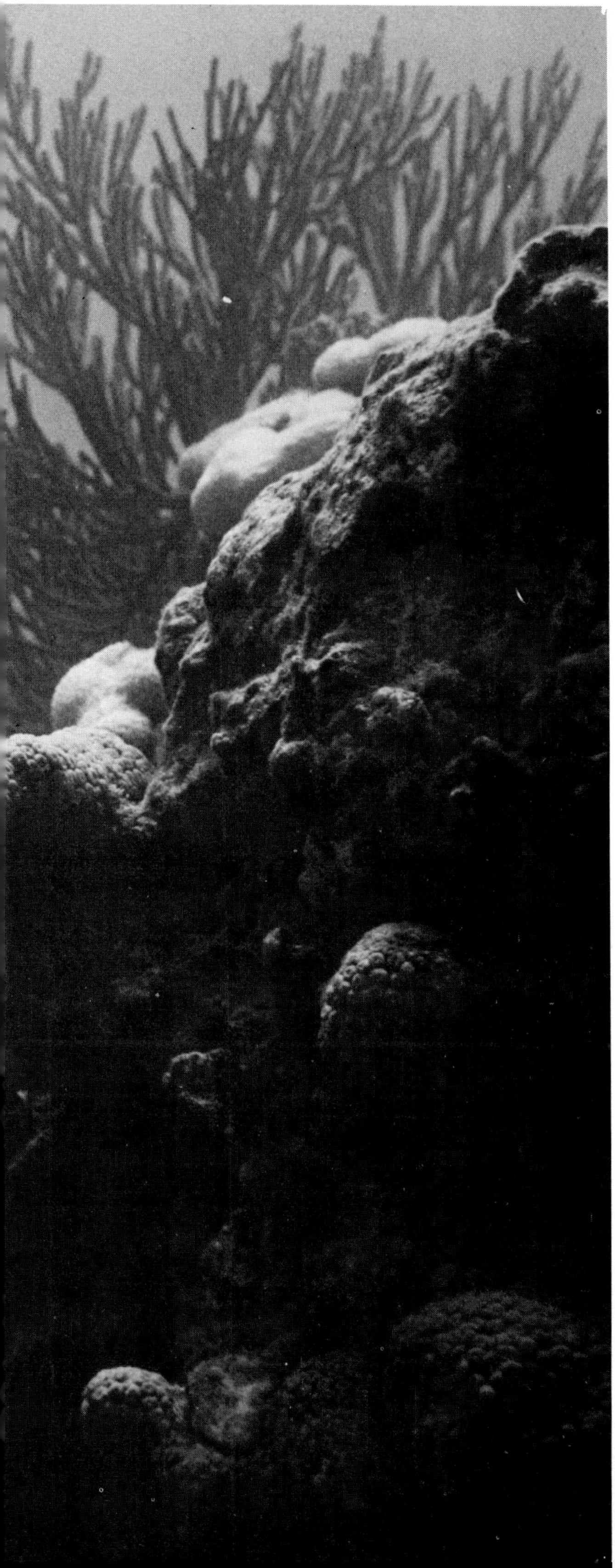
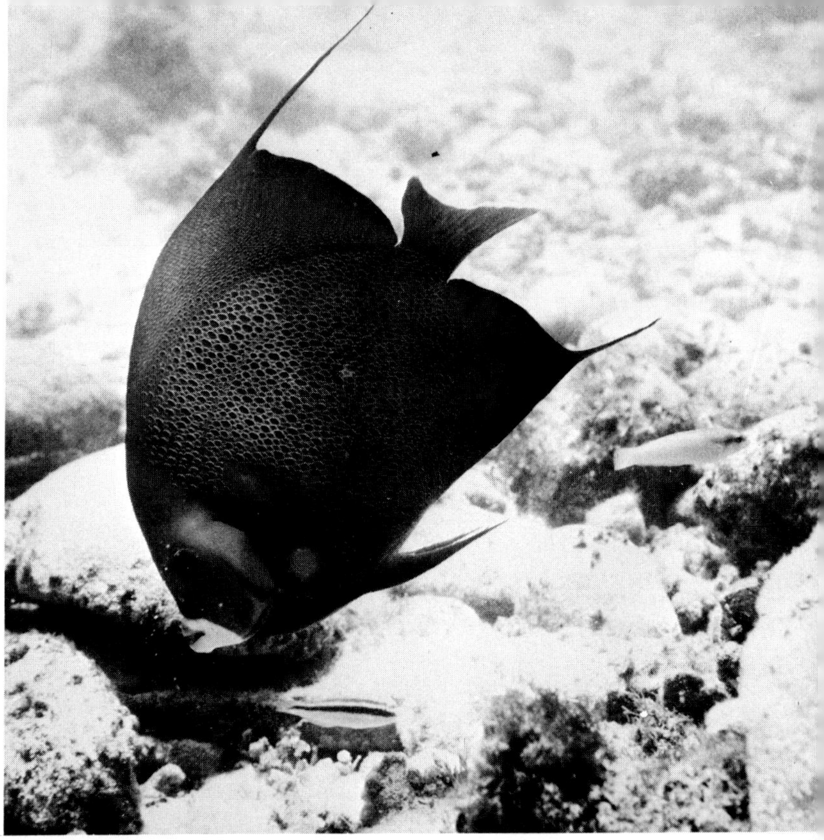
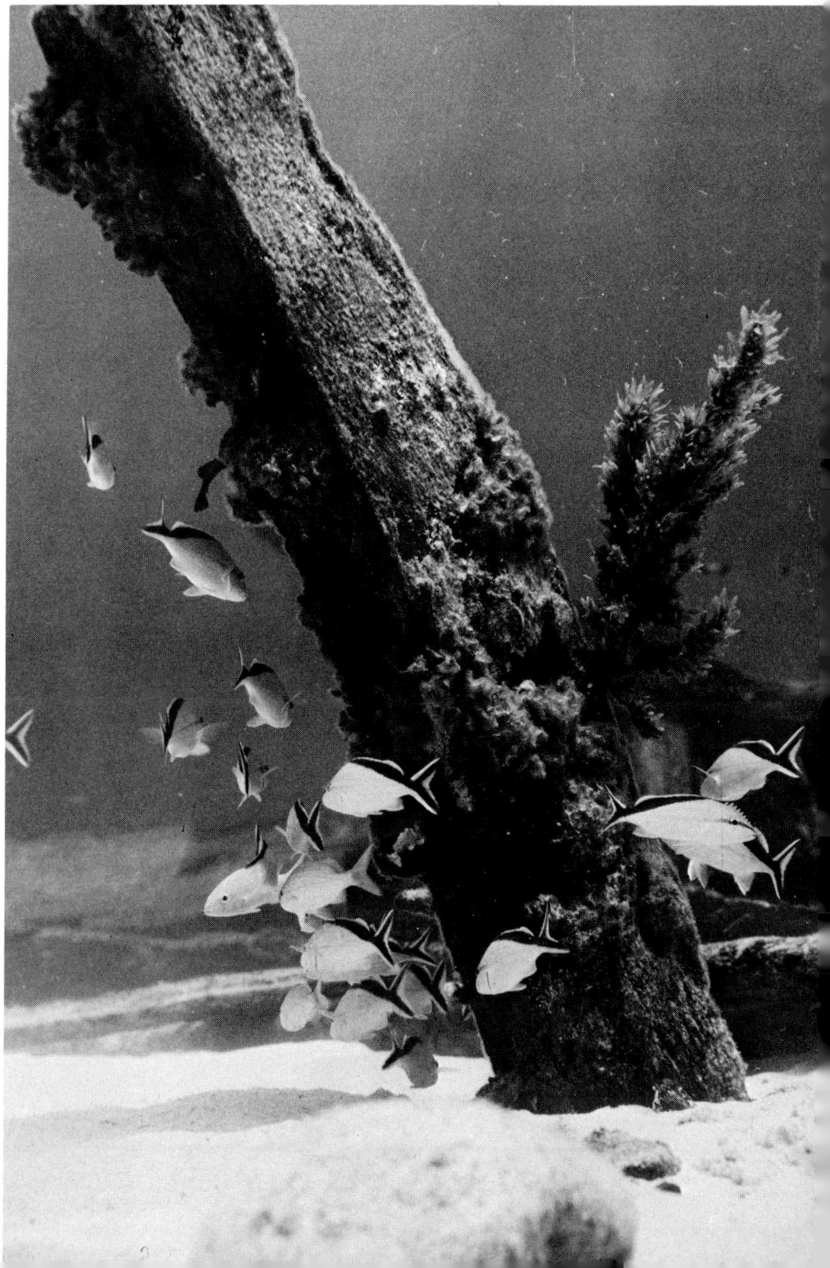

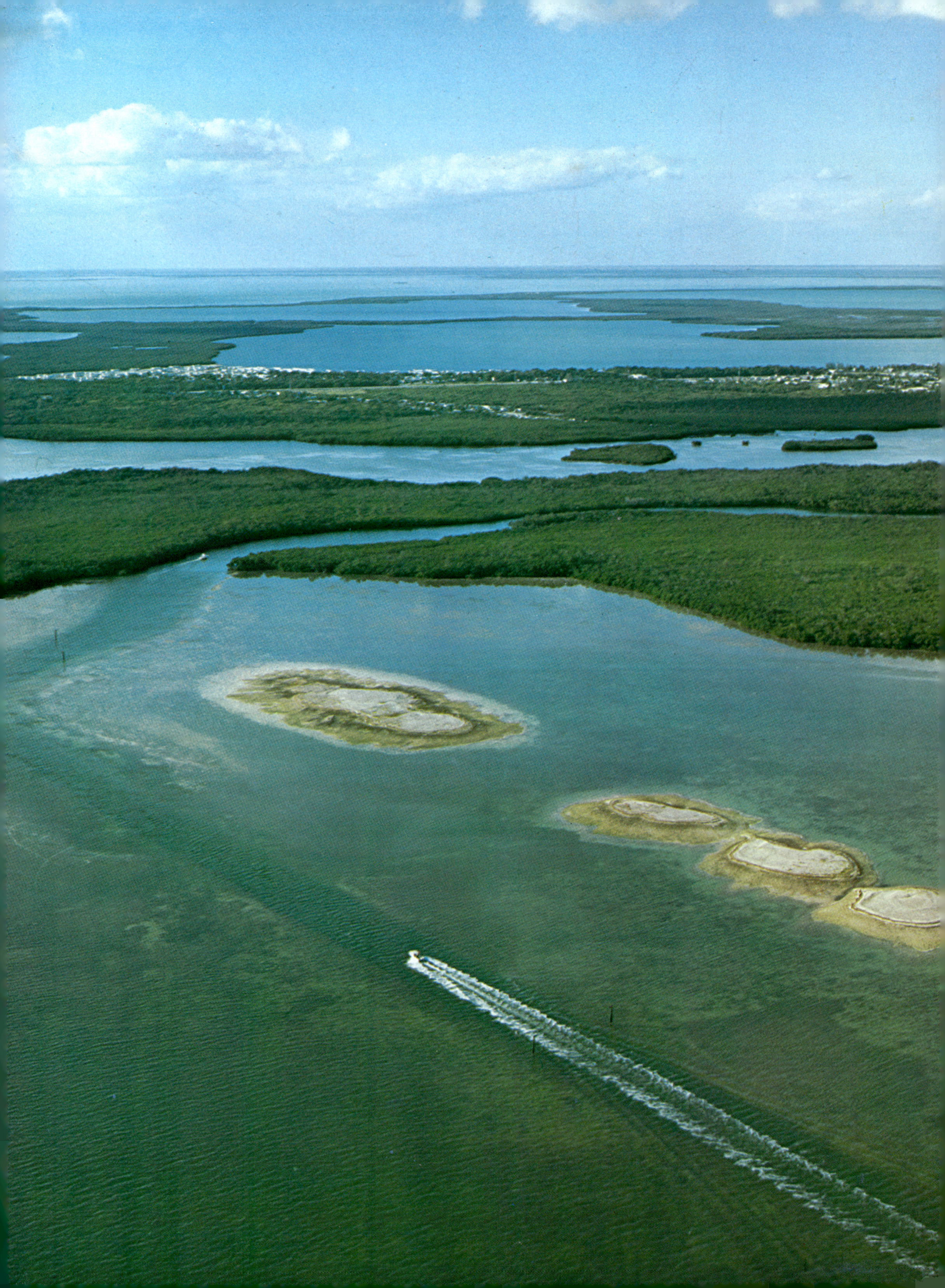

A few of the hundreds of Florida Keys can be seen in an aerial shot, *left*, which shows a motorboat's ruffled wake in the shallow waters of the Keys. *Below,* on some of the Keys, limestone rocks border the sea.

The Overseas Highway extends more than a hundred miles across the Keys, much of the way over water. *Below*, the Old Bahia Honda Bridge. *Opposite*, a nesting osprey at Cowpens Key (*top*), and an isolated beach at Casey Key (*bottom*).

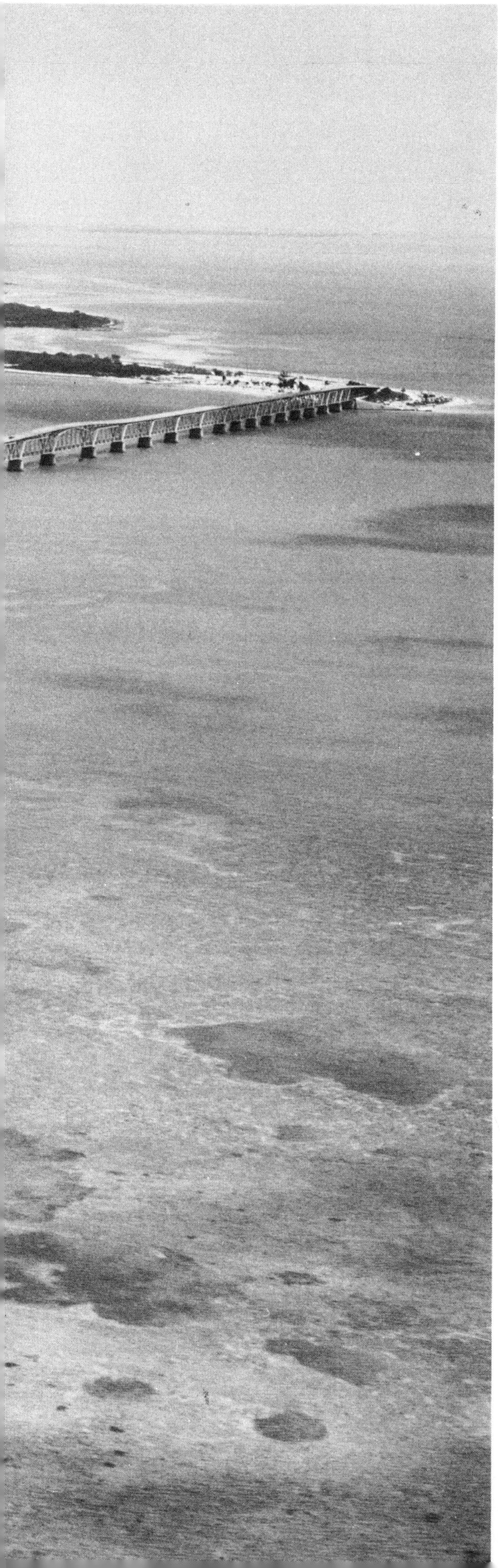

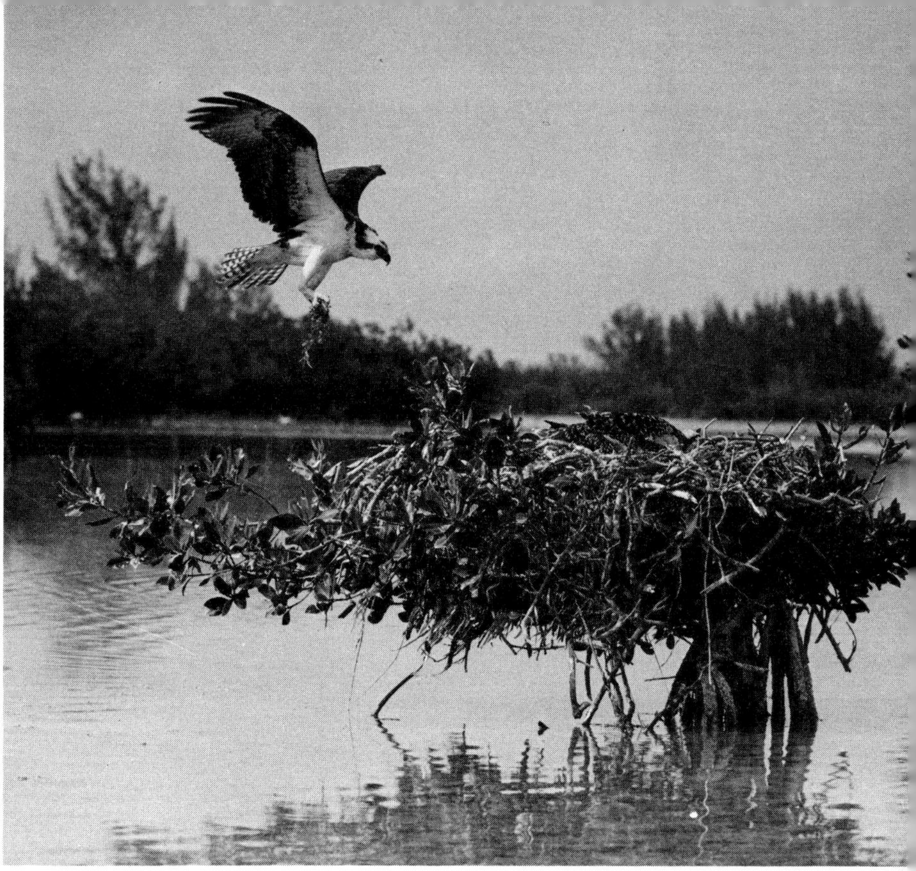

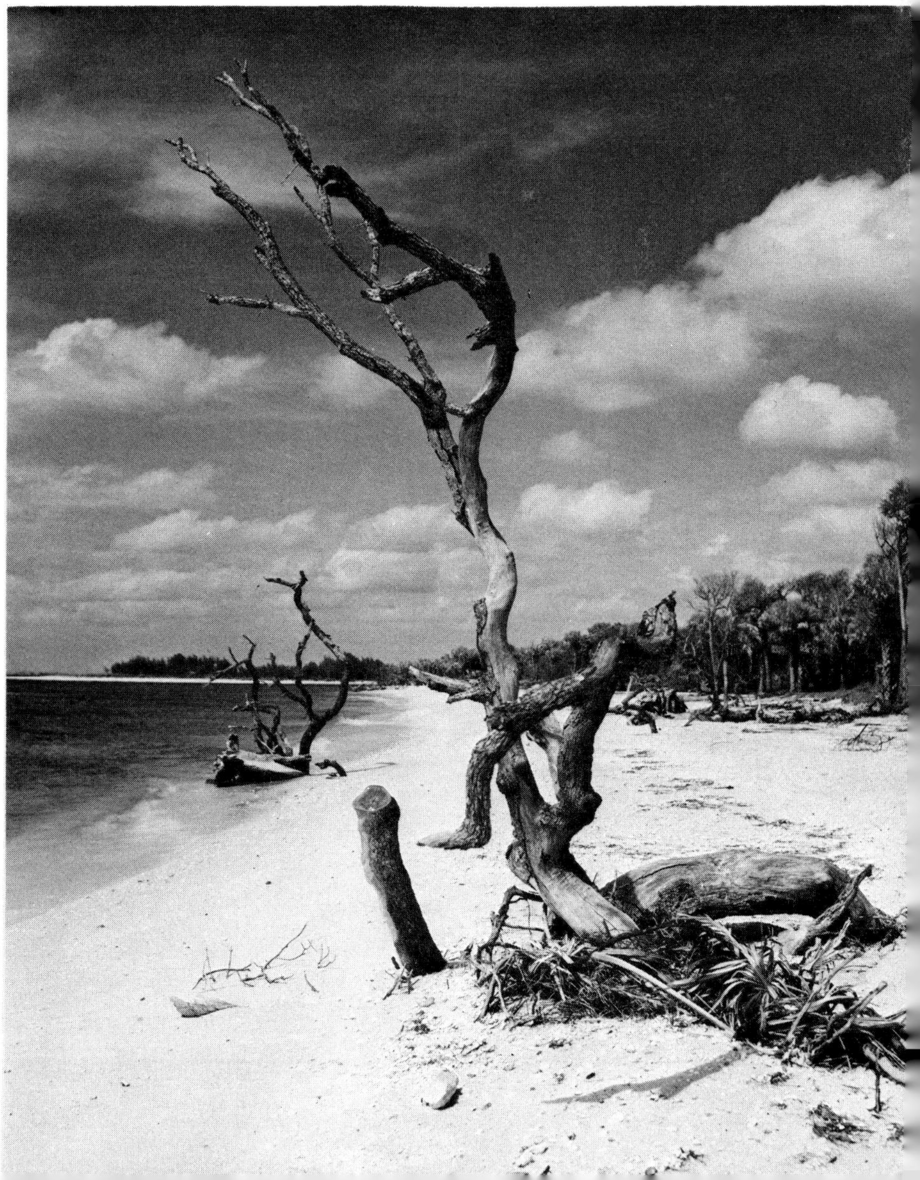

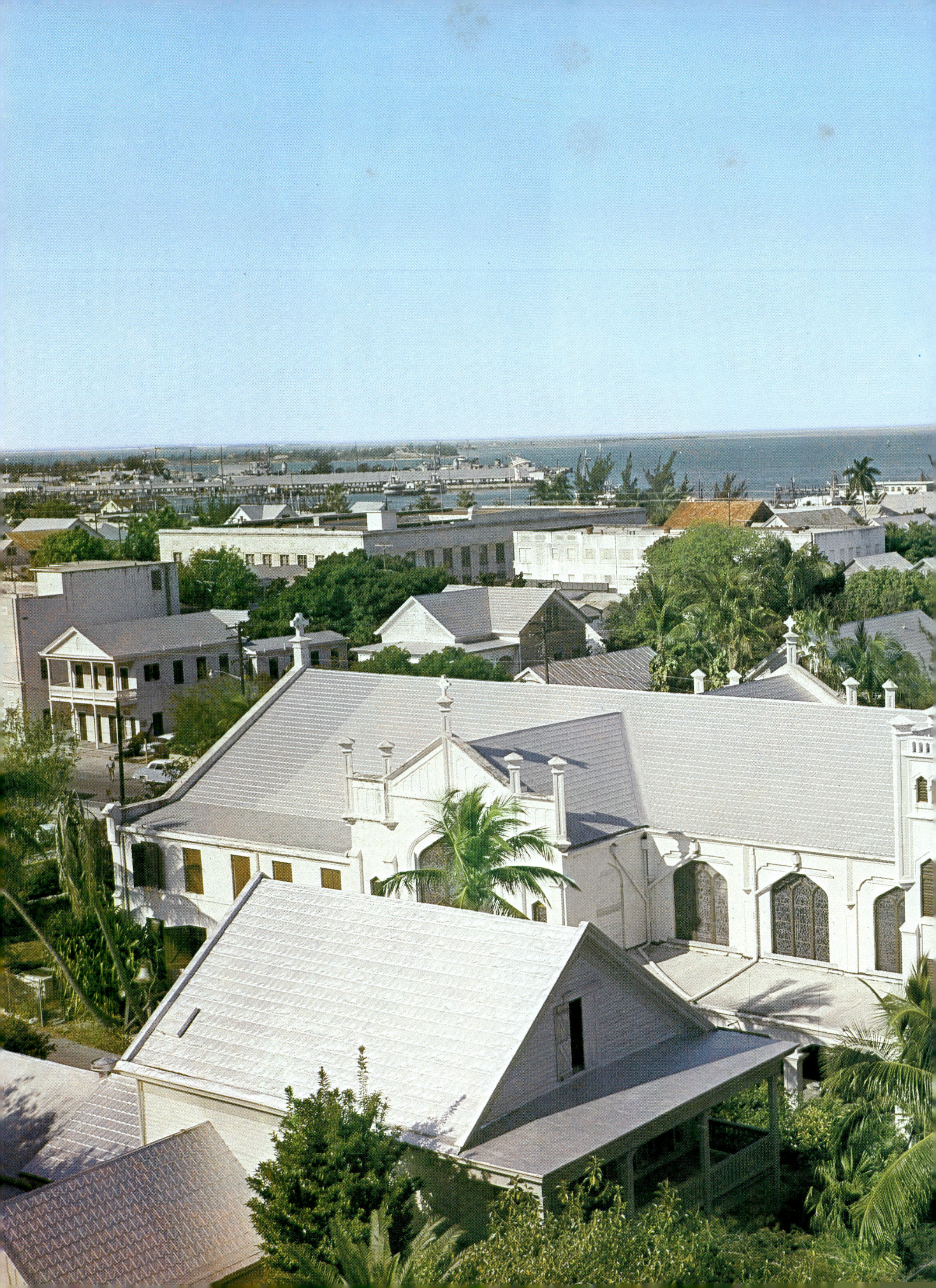

Key West, with the crisply white St. Paul's Episcopal Church in the foreground, is the southernmost city in the continental United States.

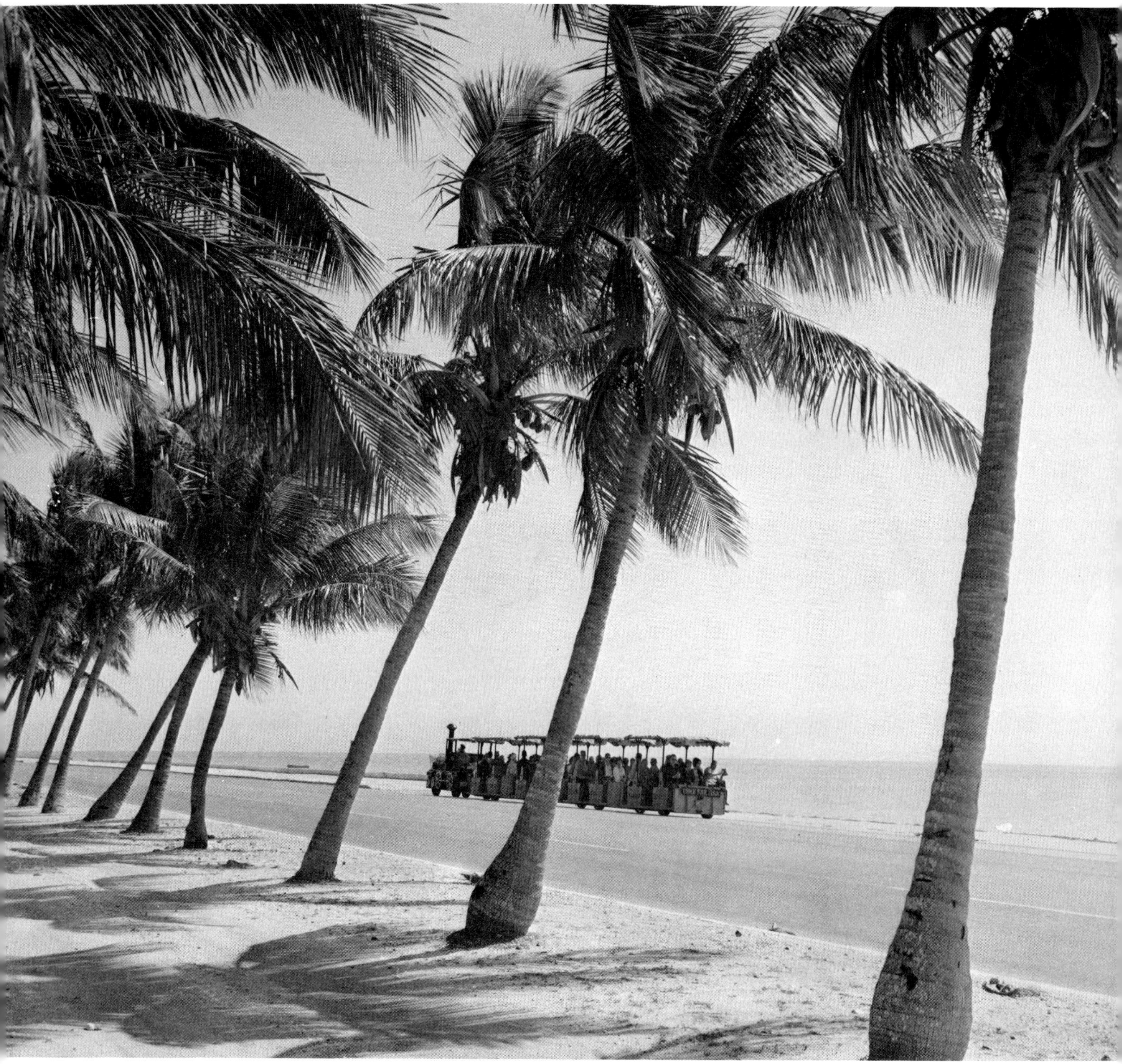

Open jitneys, *opposite*, carry tourists along Key West's Roosevelt Boulevard. *At left*, a stuffed roseate spoonbill in the house where Audubon stayed when he was in the city. *Above*, the harbor pilot's house offshore at Key West.

Overleaf: Fort Jefferson in the Dry Tortugas, seventy miles west of Key West, was begun in 1846 as part of the country's coastal defenses.

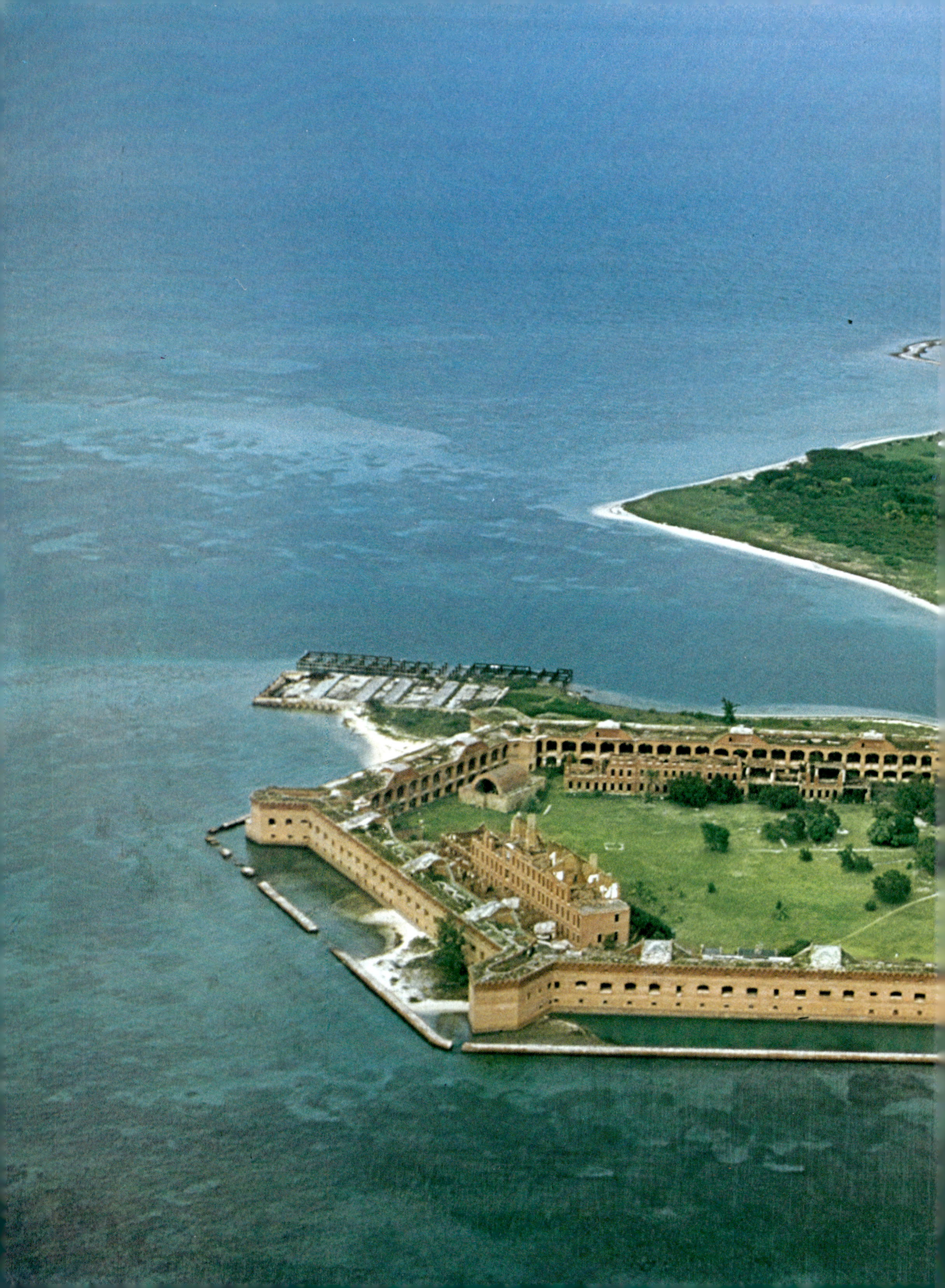

Sabal palms overlooking the Hall River near the Gulf Coast.